Beyond the Darkness

Beyond the Darkness

My Near-Death Journey to the Edge of Hell

Angie Fenimore

Foreword by Betty J. Eadie

BANTAM BOOKS
New York   Toronto   London   Sydney   Auckland

BEYOND THE DARKNESS
A Bantam Book / March 1995

Library of Congress Cataloging-in-Publication Data

Fenimore, Angie.
   Beyond the darkness : my near-death journey to the edge of hell /
Angie Fenimore.
   p. cm.
   ISBN 0-553-09966-3
   1. Fenimore, Angie. 2. Christian biography—United States.
3. Near-death experiences—Religious aspects—Christianity.
4. Visions. 5. Hell. I. Title.
BR1725.F46A3 1995
209′.2—dc20   94-42240
[B]   CIP

Published simultaneously in the United States and Canada

PRINTED IN THE UNITED STATES OF AMERICA

BVG   10 9 8 7 6 5 4 3 2 1

Acknowledgments

Thank you to my parents and stepparents for your love and for your courage, selflessness, and support in the telling of some of our darkest hours together so that others might benefit.

To my sister, Toni. I am so grateful that we came into this uncertain world together. I marvel at the goodness of God to have blessed me with a lifelong friend and confidante. I can endure anything with my hand in yours.

To my children, who had the courage to come into my life. You are angels sent from God, my teachers, and the source of my greatest joy.

And to my husband, Richard, for your patience and long suffering. Because you have stood by me through the torrents of life, ours is the greatest love story of all.

Foreword

While on tour with my book *Embraced by the Light*, I am very often asked "What did you learn about Hell?" Fortunately for me, Hell was not a part of my experience, though I did witness Satan's anger at my decision to return to earth so that I could complete my mission.

Now, whereas my experience was positive, some others have not been so fortunate. Some near-death experiencers did not go toward the light as I did, but instead they were drawn into a place filled with fear and darkness.

This revealing book by Angie Fenimore is a great example of the brushes with Hell that I have heard others try to describe. It touches on many truths that I have a firm conviction of after having my own death experience. *Beyond the Darkness* shares with us Angie's discovery that "just as God and Jesus Christ are real, a being of darkness, Satan, truly exists." And that "God loves us and calls to us," but "He cannot force us to choose the light." We are given, as we come to earth, our free will to choose the right or the wrong—negative or positive. Remember, the choice is ours—to choose the light or the darkness—even for those who have experienced death. My prayer is that we *all* choose the light.

May you find out more about the light as you read this account of a woman's journey into the darkness and learn of the *love* that brought her back safely into the light and the love of God.

Macooa ("A Piece of My Heart"),

Betty J. Eadie

Beyond the Darkness

PROLOGUE

I t would overwhelm me every January and June—that terrible state that I came to think of as "the cycle." It would begin with a sensation of emptiness, which would soon be filled by obsessive ruminations: *Grown-ups do terrible things to little girls . . . their filthy, selfish, poisoning hands, defiling . . . filling me with toxic hate. . . .* To shut out the thoughts, I dimmed my senses, fuzzed out my emotions, until I was consumed by a profound apathy, barely able to concentrate on life going on around me or to care about my husband and my two young sons. So locked up in myself, I would start to feel suffocated, choking, desperate to break out of the prison of my anxiety and despair.

The counselors I saw would spin theories about the timing, but therapy brought me no relief. My horrible secrets were so deeply buried in me that everyday life was almost a parallel, an entirely separate reality from my internal world. Even as a child I had believed that I inhabited two different spheres, convincing myself that I had been abducted by aliens from outer space and ensconced in an exact replica of my house, my school, and my world, peopled by cloned impostors who pretended to be my family and friends. Later on, I abandoned the science fiction scenario, coming to think instead that the alien being existed inside of me, an evil presence that I despised but was powerless to expel.

And so in January 1991, deep in the darkness of the cycle, I penned a note for my husband, Richard, my sister, Toni, and my sons: *"Richard, keep my wedding rings and give each of the boys one of my pearl earrings. Please, always tell Alex and Jacob how much I loved them and that this is not their fault. I can't do this anymore. Something is terribly wrong inside of me. Toni, take the silver earring. I'm sorry that I have nothing else to give you. I love you. Please understand. I just can't do this anymore."*

■

The only way out I could see was to take my life.

ONE

hen my own troubles started, I looked back to life with my family, struck by the sense that I was passing on problems that had plagued us for generations. My dad had grown up on a farm in Indiana during the Depression, the fifth of nine children who had to share one toothbrush, two beds, and their rigid father's wrath. Dad remembers that nearly every day he had to cut a switch or bring the lard paddle to Grampa in order to get a lickin', even for trivial offenses. He would be similarly overbearing, though not as harsh, with his children from his first marriage. My mother's family was also troubled—her father drank, and her mother left her twin daughters to fend for themselves. In turn, my own mother would try to escape her life, and so in time would I.

Even the story of my parents' meeting, which on the surface sounds romantic, seemed to set the stage for future sadness. They had met in a little coffee shop in Indianapolis. My mother didn't have enough change to pay the cashier, and so my dad covered her bill. My father had just been through a divorce and lost his teenage children to his first wife. My mother was looking for her ticket out of a difficult home—someone to take care of her—and my dad was looking for someone to take care of. And so in short order, I was conceived, when my mother was still just a child herself. She was only seventeen.

By the time I was born, they had moved to a tiny trailer in Phoenix, Arizona. Right from the start, I was the light of my daddy's life. By then he had mellowed, gaining a greater dimension of tenderness and affection than he had been able to express with his first family, and since my mother knew nothing of caring for a baby, it fell to him to love and pamper me. I squalled every moment that I wasn't being rocked, and so Dad rocked me and rocked me. Finally Grandma Carver, my mom's mother, came and put an end to that nonsense. Dad says it broke his heart, but the two women let me cry and made him go to bed because he was spoiling me so badly.

Most of my "memories" are family stories that were told and retold over the years. It's part of our family legend that when I learned to stand, to talk a little, and to sleep at night, I would wake up my dad in the morning. Standing in my crib, I would shake the bars and holler, "Da! Da! Da!" until he came to rescue me. But once I learned to climb, I no longer waited for Daddy to free me from my crib. One night he woke up at about three A.M. to an urgent pounding at the front door. When he answered, I was with a nice police officer who said that he'd found me playing in the dirt. From then on, Daddy would check on me periodically throughout the night to be sure I was safe in bed, not wandering down the street with a stray dog, which was another distressing habit of mine.

Still, I managed to slip out now and then. There was a night when my panicked parents found me missing from my crib and woke up half the neighborhood to search for me, with no luck. Terrified, my parents went home to call the police, but when Daddy turned on the living-room light to dial the telephone, he found me—there in the fireplace, fast asleep with my blanket. I must have heard that tale a thousand times.

Now when I think of those stories, I have to laugh. It's almost as if I were trying to escape my life, even then!

While I was Daddy's little girl first, I had three favorite companions. Two of them were my imaginary friends, Ega and Ebber, and the third was my blanket. (I have to count my blanket because I spent so much time with it and because I loved it so much.) Dad says that I would have tea parties with Ega and Ebber, but what I remember especially was their handy ability to take the rap for minor misdeeds. For example, on the coffee table in our living room was a pair of little wooden shoes that Daddy had brought back from Europe after the war. I loved those little shoes, and occasionally I would slip them on my feet and sneak out of the house to play. When I got caught, I always blamed the escape on poor Ega and Ebber. Those two friends disappeared about the time my little sister, Toni, arrived but I continued to cling to my blanket. Thick and red, it had once covered my parents' bed. It was my greatest source of comfort.

My little family—Daddy, Mama, me, and Toni—were fairly isolated in Arizona. Except for a few dissenters in California and Michigan, both sides of my family—as well as my half-siblings from Daddy's first marriage, who by then had children of their own—lived in Indiana. I saw them only a few times during my childhood, growing to love them in an innocent, abstract way, without really knowing them. But I could see that, like my father, both sets of my grandparents had grown tender with age, more indulgent and kindly with us than they had been with their own children. I remember lots of laughter during visits with Mama's family. The grandchildren would take turns on Grandpa Carver's old tire swing until we got tired or the sun went down and we couldn't see to push each other. Toni and I loved our cousins and vowed that we would all be friends for life. Chasing fireflies with Toni and my cousins, while the grown-ups sat in lawn chairs drinking beer and gabbing, is still vivid in my mind.

Daddy's family was more proper and stiff, but then they were all much older, except for Carrie and Chris, the twin daughters of Daddy's youngest brother. They were five years older than me. Carrie was born with a hole in her heart that had been patched when she was two, and so she grew up small and weak. Still, she and Chris used to give us piggyback rides around the old family farm. I remember clinging to Carrie's thin frame as she trotted across the grass, gazing across the road where acres of velvet corn field shimmered and danced in the breeze. Carrie made it over the dirt road and through to the corn, stopping to rest along the way, while Toni and Chris whizzed past. Bouncing farther down Carrie's back with each step, I started to worry that I might be dropped. Finally, I demanded to ride with Chris, regardless of whose feelings I hurt. Carrie was just too frail.

The summer that the twins were eleven years old, Carrie was hospitalized. We were visiting in Indiana then, but I never realized how sick she was. I just kept wishing she'd get well enough to play with us. But instead, she had to undergo heart surgery, and to our horror, she didn't make it through the operation. I remember being as confused as I was grief-stricken. Carrie was the first person I had ever known who died.

I remember Mama standing in Grandma Carver's living room ironing her white blouse for the funeral. "I want to come too," I protested, but Mama insisted that I was too young. "No," she said gently, "you and Toni are going to stay here with Grandma Carver." So I was left to wonder and worry: Did Carrie have to die? What did dying mean? Would I ever see her again?

Mama must have been looking for some answers, too, because after Carrie's death she started dressing us up every Sunday to try out a different church. It was my first real taste of religion, and I loved it. At the Lutheran church, Toni and I made construction paper cutouts of Easter eggs and sang and heard about God. I couldn't have been older than five or six, but I still remember the peace and security that I felt when I was told that God loves me.

Our best friends, Mary and Susie, who lived next door, were devout Catholics. They went to Catholic school and attended mass at a tall, ornate church that was both ominous and compelling. Whenever we passed it in the car, I would peer out the window, mystified by the impenetrable fortress. When we were invited to attend Mary's first communion, I was thrilled that finally I'd get to enter the wrought-iron gates and see what lay inside the forbidding stone walls—secrets so profound that my friends accepted them without question.

But the mass itself baffled me. I followed along as everyone stood up and sat down, trying to make sense of the mysterious service with its strange words and complicated rules. When it was time to go home, I had more questions than I did before we arrived. How disappointing! I wasn't even sure if the Catholics worshiped the same God as the Protestants.

My next round of religious experiments started when I was seven, after we moved to Las Vegas. The only girl in the neighborhood close to my age was Shannon, whose family was Baptist. Mom and Daddy had taken to sleeping in on Sunday mornings, so for a while Toni and I tagged along to church with Shannon's family. Later, feeling tremendously grown-up and independent, we got to ride the church bus by ourselves to Sunday school and services. I loved Sunday school, especially the Bible stories and prayers, but the service was something else. The part when the preacher got up and wailed scared the daylights out of me.

When school started, I made a new friend, Terilyn. She belonged to our car pool, which brought about my introduction to Mormonism. On Wednesday afternoons, her church held "Primary," which was like Sunday school, with lots of singing, stories about Jesus, and prayers offered by the children. Since we drove right by their church on the way home from school, Terilyn started inviting me to come along to Primary. I was drawn to the Mormons' bright, simple chapel and their conception of an accessible, loving God. I liked being able to learn about God during the week, so I could skip the scary Baptist Sunday service altogether.

One afternoon in the car pool, I mentioned that I didn't really know what to say in a prayer. Terilyn's mom explained that when we talk to God, we should always say thank you for our blessings, and we should end the prayer by saying, "In the name of Jesus Christ, Amen." The formula was that simple, which was such a big help! It freed me to talk to God, and now He became a real presence to me.

I was fascinated by God and had a desire to know Him in the close, personal way that so many of my friends knew Him. In the process of getting there, I was certainly adopting quite a religious collage, but going to church gave me a real sense of *belonging*. I loved it when the congregation sang, "He's got the whole world in His hands." I took it literally and felt so comforted by the idea of being in God's embrace.

TWO

y mother's searching, meanwhile, had gone beyond exploring churches. She had started taking psychology classes at the college. Having married so young—and having terrible fears of being out in public—she had never braved higher education. At school she made new friends who encouraged her to see a Dr. Ryefield, who could help her overcome her phobias. He was a therapist in Vegas who held group therapy sessions and ran a year-round retreat in the mountains north of the city for people who had serious problems.

At first her therapy seemed to be helping. It wasn't long after Mama started attending "group" that she got a job and a car of her own. She had a beautiful voice and was an accomplished guitarist, but she rarely shared her talent with anyone except our family because she so feared performing. But now, though, when she and Daddy went to parties or had people over to our house, Mama would take out her guitar and sing. For the first time she was able to stand being the center of attention. In fact, she really seemed to enjoy it.

That's when Mama and Daddy started fighting. It seemed that every time they talked about Mama's therapy, the discussion turned into an argument about her independence. It was the early 1970s, a time when so many people, especially women, were reaching out, looking for different ways to live. "That damn Ryefield," Daddy would growl, sure that Mama's therapy was to blame for her newfound ambitions.

"This has nothing to do with him," Mama would insist. Stabbing her finger into her chest, she would say, "I need to do something for me."

I still remember the fight that marked the crisis point in their marriage. Toni and I were sitting together in a stuffed orange chair watching TV. I tried to ignore my parents' verbal scuffling, but their anger scared me—not even so much the force of it, but what it seemed to mean for my family. I could feel the approach of disaster.

Mama was hurtling a round of demands at Daddy, along with a string of psychological theories. Toni and I looked at each other and then made a dash for the back door.

It wasn't until the following Sunday afternoon that we found out what had been so volatile. Toni and I were playing in the living room when Daddy called us to come out to the back porch, where Mama was sitting at the picnic table. Mascara stained her cheeks, and I knew she had been crying. It seemed that she had been crying a lot.

Toni and I plopped down on the bench next to Mama while Daddy took the bench across from us. When he took off his glasses and pinched the bridge of his nose, I could tell he was about to cry. I had never seen him so upset, and anxiety seemed to rise in my throat. My daddy had always been my rock-solid anchor, the one who calmed my fears. I flashed on waking up crying from a nightmare during a bout with the flu, and Daddy jumping out of bed to comfort me, twisting his leg and breaking his ankle. Unable to walk, he had crawled to my bedroom, then yanked himself up with his one good leg so I wouldn't be scared by the sight of him on his hands and knees. Turning on my light, he hopped two steps to the foot of my bed and sat down and gasped, "Uh-oh, Angie, I think I'm sicker than you," before he passed out from the pain.

Daddy was the one who had always made things all right. But now his gravelly voice broke as he told us, "Mama is going away for the summer."

My head started spinning and the tension in my throat gripped tighter, as if Daddy's words were strangling me. The pleasant warmth in the breeze felt hot and suffocating. The impossible words burned my ears. We looked to Mama, but she was crying, her hand shielding her eyes. We so rarely saw her cry.

Fighting tears, Toni and I burst out in unison, "But why!"

"Dr. Ryefield has a camp up in the mountains where they have group therapy. This is going to make Mama happy," Daddy said.

"Why can't we go too?" I asked.

"She has to go alone," Daddy said.

Toni was already crying, and I know my voice quavered as I asked, "Can we visit?"

"No," Daddy said. "We can't visit because that's part of Mama's therapy. There isn't a phone, and we can't write letters either."

"But what are we going to do?" I asked. I burst into tears, and then Daddy couldn't hold it in anymore.

"Don't you love each other anymore?" Toni sobbed.

"Of course we do," he told us. "It's just for the summer, and this is going to help Mama learn how to be a better mother to you girls."

Mama remained silent. She seemed too upset to speak. Daddy got up from the picnic table and moved over to the lawn chair on the back porch. Calling Toni and me to come and sit on his lap, he tried to console us through his own tears. The three of us rocked and cried there together for an hour.

Later I sat on my parents' bed to watch Mama pack for her trip. I was swirling with confusion; so angry, so frightened, so sad. Inside me a whispering voice hinted to me that this crisis was the threshold of pandemonium in my life. I could feel Mama's tension, and I wanted to ease it, to bind her with my love. Sliding off the bed, I went to find my red blanket to soothe her and remind her of home. I presented it to her, almost sacrificially declaring, "Here, Mama. You can take this with you."

Mama bent down and kissed me, but she seemed distracted. "No, you keep your blanket, honey," she said.

"No," I insisted, "you take it with you. I don't need it anymore."

In the end, she accepted it.

■

And so it was just the three of us now. Every night Daddy took us out to eat, mostly to fast-food restaurants, which we loved at first. Then when we got home, Daddy would haul out the vodka while Toni and I went to play outside until the streetlights came on. That was the only rule that we still adhered to, and only because we were afraid of the dark. Most nights Daddy would drink and cry until he passed out.

I was the oldest, and I could see that I would have to be the parent in our house for a while. Of course, with the maturity and skills of a nine-year-old, I couldn't keep house like Mama did, but I could watch out for Toni and try to make Daddy happy. Toni and I did our best to cheer him up. We truly worshiped him, and we knew that our love could sustain him.

One night, when Daddy had passed out, slumped in a chair in the living room, we concocted a special surprise. Toni and I constructed a crown from a paper bag, which we covered with tin foil, and I crayoned a colorful sign that read "King Daddy." Then we rummaged through our toy box filled with tattered "dress-up" clothes and pulled out an old satin nightgown of Mama's, which we draped over Daddy's shoulders. After a little ceremony we crowned "King Daddy" and took turns posing next to him and snapping photos with the Polaroid camera. The next day when we woke him up, Daddy got such a kick out of our pictures.

Since regular bedtimes went out the door along with my mother, Toni and I couldn't wake up in time for the Baptist bus to Sunday school, so we started to hold our own services. We began by watching *David and Goliath*, a children's program that depicted Bible stories using animated clay figures. After that, we each delivered a Baptist sermon to each other, read from our Gideon Bible, and dropped borrowed change from Daddy's dresser into an Easter basket. Then we passed each other the Lord's supper—broken bits of bread in our best china bowls, washed down with grape juice or occasionally real wine—sang a verse of "This Little Light of Mine" or "Deep and Wide," and wound things up with a Mormon prayer.

Erratic bedtimes weren't the only sign of chaos in our lives.

I don't think I took a single bath, and I know I didn't brush my teeth all that summer. None of us had any idea of how to shop or cook or clean, though one night we did attempt a trip to the laundromat. Daddy shoveled clothes into a washing machine while I read him the instructions out loud. Nearby, a woman sat reading a magazine while waiting for her clothes to dry. Peeking over the pages, she watched Daddy read the detergent box, murmuring, "Hmmm, let's see now . . ." We must have looked awfully pitiful, for she came over to help us out.

Smiling at me and then looking up at Daddy, she said, "You know, if you mix those dark clothes with the whites, the colors are gonna bleed."

"Oh . . ." Daddy said.

Our rescuer helped Daddy sort and wash the laundry, leaving Toni and me free to explore the laundromat and play with our Barbies in the pastel chairs that were joined together with a metal bar. Finally, the wash was done—clean, dry, and folded. Our kind helper waved and said, "Bye-bye, girls. You take care of your daddy, now."

Well, we were certainly trying.

THREE

hree long months went by, and then it was time to go get Mama. Toni and I were ecstatic, jabbering excitedly as we piled into the car for the daylong drive. Once we reached the mountains, it took us a few hours to find the remote road that would take us into the canyon that lodged the retreat. It led us to a hogback where the road grew so narrow in spots that only one car could pass, and both sides of the road dropped off into steep slopes. By then it was dark, and Daddy was so worried about slipping over the edge that, as soon as we reached a place wide enough, he pulled over to wait for daylight to come.

When the sun peeked over the eastern ridge of the canyon, we started driving again. Once off the narrow road, we drove through a creek bed and finally came to the dirt track that would take us to the camp. "Look for a trailer, girls," Daddy said. Eagerly, we bounced over the seat and scrambled to the windows—Daddy's diligent helpers—fighting to get the first glimpse.

Finally, I spotted the trailer. We pulled alongside it and piled out of the car. Inside the trailer were a telephone and several cardboard boxes, as well as two nice women. One of them was to be our guide, for the camp was accessible only on foot, five long miles deeper into the brush.

So we set off plodding behind her, alternately whining and excited. It seemed that Toni asked every fifteen minutes, "When will we get there, Daddy?"

"Pretty soon, honey," Daddy would answer patiently. Clouds of dirt, stirred up by my feet, coated my legs as I trudged down the path.

We grew so hot and dusty that the water we kept swigging from our guide's canteen barely seemed to dampen our scratchy throats. We were getting cranky when, at last, in a thicket ahead I saw a tepee hidden amid the trees. Smoke curled through the air above it. We rounded a corner, and there in the distance was a shallow basin, with trees scattered across one side. We had arrived. Bear Creek!

Our guide directed us to a tepee tucked between a few patches of trees. Some people with long hair came out, dressed in ragged jeans. One of them was Mama! She looked so different, but her hair and clothes weren't all that had changed about her. Even as she hugged us and said that she missed us, there was an unmistakable apathy about her. Mama had always been aloof, but through my excitement at seeing her, it chilled me that she was so withdrawn.

One of the men seemed to be in a position of authority because he coaxed Daddy into the tent with Mama and himself, saying that there was a matter that they had to discuss.

Daddy looked tense, and I could tell that he didn't like these new people, but he shrugged his shoulders and complied.

When he came out, Daddy looked dejected. He was silent as Mama showed us around the camp. There were only two buildings—the cook-shack, which was a large log structure on stilts where meals were eaten on tables made from logs—and the meeting house, an octagonal building with benches built along the inside walls where camp residents held group therapy. Everyone lived in tepees. Some tepees were larger than others, but most accommodated two or three adults. Mama's excitement rose when we climbed the hill behind the cook-shack to her tepee, which her female tentmate had vacated so that we could all stay there. It was as if Toni and I were her sisters and Mama was showing us her dorm room at college. She presented us with gifts of polished stones. Toni's was a rich, shiny brown with sparkling amber streaks. "This reminds me of you, Toni," she said. "So calm and easygoing." Mine was a swirl of colors, almost a paisley print of lavender, vermilion, and smoky green. I was so touched by her choice. I'd never thought that she had seen beyond my bubbly veneer to the world of my imagination.

Soon the big cowbell rang for dinner, and we met the rest of the community over gloppy soybean and tomato stew—not my idea of a good meal. Luckily there was dessert, a birthday cake, that I could fill up on. The birthday girl was Danielle, one of the "permanent" children, who was there without her parents and shared a tepee with an adult woman. When a woman rose to announce that it was time to sing "Happy Birthday," she laughed, saying that Danielle was getting a lot of attention lately. Leaning over, I asked my mother what she meant. "Oh, Danielle started her period last week and we gave her a party,"

Mama said. I was so embarrassed, shocked that my formerly ordinary mother would treat something that private so casually, out loud, with a group that included men.

The next day we met another of the permanent children, Davey. We happened upon him while exploring the woods. He was wearing only filthy underwear and had a profound speech impediment. He was obviously malnourished and socially starved. As the other children explained, Davey was allowed only one meal of bread and water a day. He was forbidden to associate with any of the adults and was only allowed limited contact with the children because he was undergoing "deprivation therapy." Even at nine years old, I knew that something was seriously wrong with how this boy was being treated.

But the shock of seeing Davey paled that evening when Daddy told us the results of the conference he'd had upon our arrival. Mama would be staying longer because she hadn't "resolved all of her issues." She wouldn't be coming home with us.

■

And so the journey that had begun so exuberantly ended in a cloud of depression.

We would return to Bear Creek to visit Mama a few more times. On our next trip I saw an older boy in front of the cook-shack, where he was practicing throwing a knife into the ground. I didn't recognize him, so I sat down on the steps to chat. "What's your name?" I asked.

"Billy," he said through the lit cigarette hanging from his lips. He continued to throw the knife and retrieve it.

"How old are you?" I asked.

"Sixteen," he declared. His shoulder-length black hair was

pulled back into a ponytail, and his jeans were full of holes. Except for the boyish smirk on his face, he looked as if he'd lived a lot longer than sixteen years.

"So why are you at Bear Creek?" I pressed.

Billy muttered some obscenity about his parents and Dr. Ryefield. He believed that his parents and all the Bear Creek people—but especially Dr. Ryefield—were crazy.

The next day Mama told me and Toni that Billy's family had come for the weekend to work out some of their hostility. She suggested, and Daddy insisted, that we stay away from the camp buildings. So along with the other visiting children, we took a dip in the swimming hole. Davey came with us and swam without underwear, insisting that it was better to be without clothes. A grown man joined us and also swam naked, which made Toni and me uncomfortable. Noticing our embarrassment, the others bullied us and tried to convince us to undress too. They made us feel stupid, but we clung to our clothes and our modesty.

Then we heard shouts echoing across the canyon. The noise was coming from the cook-shack. Curious and a little fearful, we all crept up the steep path, next to the waterwheel, to see what was going on.

A crowd had assembled outside the cook-shack. At its center was Billy's family, who were all wearing dog collars attached to chains. Big men in the group held the chains to keep the family members apart as they lashed out—growling, barking, and screaming obscenities—at each other, as the onlookers cheered them on. I had never seen such an explosion of violent adult rage, and I found the scene shocking and surreal. The father and the oldest brother were the fiercest, spitting at each other, clawing the air as if they were going to tear each other apart. I was sure that they would rip through their bonds and wreak havoc on us all, to match the emotional destruction they were wreaking on each other. Suddenly I realized how strange and isolated Bear Creek really was.

The next time I went to visit, the group had taken Billy's shoes and shaved his head because he had tried to run away. They thought that would keep him there. When I tried to ask him how he was, he just glanced at me and looked away. He couldn't trust anybody. He had been broken.

But for me the worst experience came over the Thanksgiving holiday weekend. Mama had spent a few days with us in Vegas, and Toni and I had come back with her, leaving Daddy behind. By then we had befriended several of the other children, and a group of us set off to play with Davey, who was still in isolation. When the cowbell rang for Thanksgiving dinner, Davey begged us to bring him some food. The others were afraid to do it, but I couldn't leave him alone and hungry on Thanksgiving. So I whispered that he should hide under the cook-shack, and filling my dinner plate an extra time, I would sneak it out to him. It was dark when I smuggled out the food, but one of the other children spotted me, and being an obedient child, she told her mother about it.

The next morning, Toni and I were summoned to the group therapy session, where it was announced that I had violated one of the laws of the community. Dr. Ryefield proposed that I be punished for my crime, but not without first asking my mother if she approved.

I looked to Mama, confident that she would shield me from such injustice. I could feel the hot stares of everybody in the room. I knew deep inside that I had made the right choice in feeding Davey, but still I felt guilty and ashamed—not for feeding him, but because I knew that my mother thrived on these people's admiration. I worried that my crime would bring shame on her. When Mama turned to look at me for a moment, I could see in her eyes that she, too, was tormented by my public humiliation. But when she finally spoke, all Mama said was, "Yes, that's fair."

I was deprived of my next meal as penance, but the far worse punishment was my mother's betrayal and my sense that these people had stolen her from me. As the community ate lunch together—I sat there without a plate—I could tell that Mama was uneasy about what had happened during group. She kept glancing at me and finally asked, "Are you okay, Ang?"

"I'm not even hungry," I said, trying to hide my embarrassment and wishing that she hadn't called more attention to the fact that I wasn't eating. I could see now that there wasn't room for Toni and me in her life, really. It was us or Bear Creek and she had chosen. We had lost her.

FOUR

D addy now realized that Mama was gone for good and tried to cushion our despair. I didn't even know what a divorce was. The legal intricacies were beyond me, and it filled me with dread even to try to imagine Mama's permanent absence from our home.

Daddy's efforts to fill the emptiness became a nightmare for Toni and me. Most of the women he went out with resented sharing him with us and feared the responsibilities of our "instant family." Brandy was different. She was a voluptuous nineteen-year-old receptionist from Daddy's office, who had long blond hair and wispy bangs. She was married, but her husband was the one who orchestrated her involvement with my Dad, and I'm still not sure what longings this triangle satisfied in each of them. Since Brandy knew that we were important to Daddy, she was very nice to us. One time she took us to a fabric store, offering to make us pantsuits out of any fabric we liked. I chose brown cotton with pictures of candy bars all over it. Even though our pantsuits never fit well, we wore them all the time. We needed Brandy's attention and kindness even more than we needed clothes.

Brandy lived with her husband, Sonny, and a big, smelly man named Lenny in a horrid little trailer in North Las Vegas. Sonny had been to prison and wore his cigarettes rolled up in his T-shirt sleeve. He rarely spoke directly to us, for which we were grateful, but his leering eyes would fix on me while he commented to Lenny about what "hot chicks" Toni and I were going to be in a year or two.

One Friday night Daddy took Toni and me out for burgers and then announced that we were going to Brandy's place for the evening. "I don't want to go," I protested. I hated Sonny and Lenny.

"Oh, we won't stay too long," Daddy replied, brushing off my complaints.

Old newspapers and empty beer cans littered the living room of the trailer. There was a glass tank about the size and depth of my little inflatable swimming pool in the corner of the room. It was filled with water, rocks, and algae, surrounded by heat lamps. In the tank Brandy and Sonny kept the two baby alligators that were Lenny's companions. Even though it meant being left alone with Lenny and the hissing gators, I was a little relieved when Brandy took Dad and menacing-looking Sonny and disappeared into the bedroom.

Toni and I sat nervously, glued side by side on the worn velour couch, while Lenny flipped through dirty magazines. Occasionally he was moved to share his favorite pictures with us. We were too uncomfortable and miserable to say a word.

A few hours passed before Dad emerged from the bedroom, ready to take us home. He was very drunk. In the car Toni slept across the passenger seat, but I stayed awake on Daddy's lap. I had to help him steer.

Not long afterward, Brandy disappeared from our lives. Daddy was evasive about the reason, but Toni and I surmised that Sonny had begun to feel squeezed out of Daddy and Brandy's relationship, that the triangle had started to capsize. To punish Brandy, Sonny had stabbed her horse to death. That was enough to open Daddy's eyes.

A series of tawdry women and sometimes their men continued to traipse through our lives. When Dad dated, Toni and I would be left with sitters or, not infrequently, be dragged along. With the confusion of neglect and drunken parties came the sexual abuse that haunted me for years to come. I hate even to remember, never mind describe, those encounters and the feelings they sparked in me—the terror, the sense of being too fragile to resist, the conspiracy of silence that kept me from seeking help, the belief that I had brought those painful attentions on myself, the guilt and shame and self-blame. I have since learned that such feelings are common among survivors of sexual abuse. But at the time I was so completely alone and afraid that I could turn my anger only on myself, shrouding my brittle sense of self with abject worthlessness.

That was when the nightmares and eating disorders began. The food I ate was the only thing in life I could control. I remember one night when we went out to eat at Denny's—fast food was still our mainstay. Nothing sounded appealing, but I ordered anyway. I took a small bite of potatoes and felt compelled to clean off my fork, so I folded my napkin and pulled the fork between the folds. I took another bite and wiped my fork again. I felt that dirty, that contaminated.

"What in the world are you doing?" Toni pried.

"I just don't want to mix any of my food," I said.

"But you're just eating potatoes," she replied.

"Worry about your own food and leave me alone," I snapped, and then stomped off to the bathroom until Toni and Dad were through. These peculiar rituals gave way to periods of starving myself for days at a time.

Daddy had no idea how to handle my distress and chose to overlook it, no doubt feeling guilty about the tangled mess our lives seemed to have become. Mama was barely a shadow in our lives. Having completed her treatment at Bear Creek, she had gotten a job and taken an apartment in Las Vegas with friends. She had changed her name and even had a nose job— symbols of the new woman she had become. She was too removed from us to get involved in my problems. By now I hardly referred to her as Mama even in my thoughts.

Daddy had been offered a chance to transfer to Southern California, which he gladly accepted and Mama hadn't protested. We moved from Las Vegas three years to the day after we had arrived. Our new apartment in California was dark and drab, but I saw it as a chance for me to start over too. I even changed my name, introducing myself to the neighborhood kids as Roxanne and Toni as Lorena. Our new names lasted until we were enrolled in school and our birth certificates gave us away.

Among our neighbors were two boys, Paul and Eric, who loved to annoy me and Toni. One sunny afternoon as I scribbled in the dirt, I saw the younger one, Eric, watching me through his screen door. Huge oak trees lined the sidewalk connecting the apartment houses, and I picked up a few acorns to toss at him. Undaunted, Eric smashed his nose against the screen, bellowing, "Roxanne, I want to kiss you!"

I scowled back at him. "You monkey-face snot head, stay away from me!" I yelled, rising to my feet and fleeing down the walk to the pool.

"I love you, Roxanna-banana," he squealed as he threw open the screen door and darted after me. Screaming, I ran around the block with Eric chasing behind. I made it to the parking lot and back up toward the walkway that separated our tiny yards where Eric's mother, Harriet, was standing out front, tapping her foot and drying her hands with a dish towel. I slid to a halt as Eric came tearing around the end of the apartment building.

"Eric! You get in the house this instant, and you stop bothering Roxanne!" Harriet cried. She smacked him in the rear end as he trotted past her into the little apartment.

Then she turned to me. She was the biggest woman I had ever seen, with broad shoulders and the thick physique of a linebacker. But her brown eyes were kindly when she smiled at me and said, "Is your dad still at work, honey?"

"Yeah, for another hour," I replied.

Harriet placed her hand on my shoulder and told me, "Go get your sister and come on over for some cookies."

Harriet became a new pillar in our lives. I even tolerated her obnoxious son Eric in order to spend time with her. She brought casseroles over and played matchmaker for Dad. One friend she had in mind had just been through a divorce and was in the hospital having a hysterectomy. When the friend recovered, Harriet fixed them up.

That is how we met JoAnne. So many of the women Dad was interested in didn't want to mother two little girls, and the ones who did seem to care about us didn't seem to appeal to him. But JoAnne met all of Dad's requirements. She was single, kept him happy in the bedroom and kept the house clean, had a five-year-old daughter of her own, and was willing to take on Toni and me in exchange for Dad's love. Not long after their first date, Dad and JoAnne were married.

And not long after that, the strain and tension of trying to put two families together began to wear on us all.

One afternoon, I was snooping through some things that JoAnne had piled in my closet when I discovered a manila folder. After peeking out into the hallway to be sure I was alone, I opened it. I was horrified by what I saw. Inside were pictures of JoAnne lying in a hospital bed, her eyes blackened and swollen shut. Lines of sutures held the pieces of her face together and a brace held her jaw in place. Along with the pictures were copies of insurance forms, accident reports and a newspaper article. I pored over the information: "Two vehicle accident . . . JoAnne Leigh, 20 . . . critical condition . . . 8 months pregnant, lost the baby." I quickly stashed the file back where I found it.

Some time later, JoAnne told me about her ordeal. Realizing that the baby had been killed in the crash, the doctors induced labor. It took all night, and then she started hemorrhaging. She could hear the doctors saying, "This one's not going to make it. She'll be gone in half an hour. We'd better go talk to the family." And she thought, "I can't die. I'm too young." At that moment she realized that she was floating above her body, able to see herself on the bed, the doctors frantically working, her family crying in the hallway. She was surrounded by bright light from which two beings emerged who seemed familiar, though she wasn't sure who they were. "It's not your time," they told her. "But I don't want to go back," she pleaded. They insisted, "You have to go back. The

Lord still has a purpose for you on earth." And so, she told me, she took the difficult course of returning to life to complete whatever her special duty was.

I didn't know what to think about her story, but I knew the part about having a difficult life was true. JoAnne had told me of her tortured childhood, and I knew she suffered from migraines. It wasn't until later that we learned of her bouts of clinical depression, her suicide attempts, and the violent outbursts that led to stays in the mental ward of the hospital. In fact, that's where she was when Harriet told us she was recovering from a hysterectomy.

JoAnne provided me with structure and the chance to be a little girl again, two things I desperately needed and deeply resented, and so I became the target of her wrath. Something as trivial as my forgetting to fold a load of clothes would provoke a hateful blast of accusations. JoAnne seemed convinced that everything I did wrong was meant to inconvenience her, and she would strike out, shouting that I was stupid or, worse, "just like your mother."

But her reactions were completely unpredictable. When I was on a field trip in sixth grade, I got in trouble on the school bus for throwing papers at a boy who was teasing me. As I walked home from school that afternoon, my stomach ached in anticipation of a tirade from JoAnne. I had never gotten in trouble at school before, and I was sure that JoAnne wouldn't believe that I had been defending myself. All the way home I kept trying to remember if there was anything else I'd done wrong, like forgetting to turn off the curling iron or leaving my empty cereal bowl in the sink—anything that would put her in a bad mood and make my situation worse.

When I came through the front door, I could hear her banging dishes and slamming the cupboards in the kitchen. I was in for it. Steadying myself, I went into the kitchen and laid my teacher's note on the counter, right next to JoAnne's collection of Demerol and Valium.

"What's this?" she snarled at me, picking up the note.

"I got in trouble on the bus for throwing paper at Nathan after he said I had chicken legs," I sheepishly replied.

"Did you start it?" JoAnne barked.

"No," I said.

"That idiot principal. I'll fix his wagon," she said.

I just stood there in disbelief. The next day JoAnne went to the principal and fought my case for me. I was grateful for her support, but I knew better than to count on it. JoAnne's mood swings kept me constantly off balance.

She was also kind during my second encounter with death. The call came one evening when we had just finished dinner, and Daddy answered the phone. Almost immediately he dropped it, sobbing into his hands. JoAnne picked up the phone, and I heard her say, "Okay, we're on our way."

My uncle Sam had been in a car accident on the highway between Las Vegas and California. He was heading home from a business trip and had been drinking when he crossed over the center divider and hit a semi head-on. Daddy was beside himself, but JoAnne sprang into action. Stabilizing volatile situations was her greatest gift; it was the small crises that she couldn't seem to weather. She called a neighbor to baby-sit for us, then grabbed her purse and she and Dad were gone.

Toni was crying hysterically, and so I held her and tried to reassure her. "Uncle Sam will be fine, Toni. JoAnne got into that really bad accident and she's fine," I said.

Toni pushed me away in surprise. "You dummy," she said. "Uncle Sam's dead!"

Uncle Sam's funeral was the first I was allowed to attend. I had never seen someone who was dead, and I was both curious and scared, thinking of the moment when we would walk by the casket. Toni and I walked up the aisle with Uncle Sam's daughter, Melanie, the youngest of his four children. When we reached the casket, she bent down and kissed her father, fastening a little pin, a pair of praying hands, on his lapel.

Uncle Sam's black hair shimmered, and the thick makeup on his face looked artificial. He looked just like a mannequin, I thought, with no trace of human energy or personality. It was clear to me that he was no longer in his body, that his soul had passed from him. At that moment I knew that there must be life after death.

As time went on, JoAnne's hatred of me grew. I remember one Saturday afternoon when Toni and I asked if we could take the bus to the beach. JoAnne said no, that we had too much work to do, and it was nearly four o'clock by the time we finished the chores she assigned us. So we decided to make the best of things and lie in the yard to get some sun. By then our tiny back yard was completely shadowed by the apartment house, so we set up our lawn chairs in the front yard. Spying us through the upstairs bedroom window, JoAnne flew into a rage, tearing down the stairs and throwing open the front door. "You little whore!" she screamed at me, with murder in her eyes. "I know what you're trying to do." Mortified, I didn't dare ask her what she meant for fear she would tell me and all the rest of the neighbors. I felt that she took pride in belittling and humiliating me in public. Most of the time I didn't even know what I had done to provoke her vile anger.

I did my best to stay out of JoAnne's way, to clean the house and cook, but inevitably I would do something, and her rage would erupt all over again.

One afternoon, I came home from school to find JoAnne
lying on the couch with her heavy, drugged arm draped across
her face. The curtains were pulled tight, so I knew that she
must have a migraine. "Shut that damned door," she bawled.
As usual, her shouting made my stomach burn and my lungs
clutch with fear. If I slipped quietly through the room, she
would think that I didn't care that she was in pain, but if I
asked how she was, I would invite a new barrage of insults.
Either way, I might provoke her to another suicide attempt.
Gently pushing the door closed, struggling with my options, I
caught a glimpse of papers scattered across the kitchen floor. I
tiptoed across the carpet to investigate. There on the floor lay
all of our family photos, some tattered and torn, some burned.
In each photo, my image had been obliterated.

Terrified, I disappeared into my room until Dad came
home. I could hear them arguing back and forth.

"Good grief, JoAnne. What in the world possessed
you . . ." Daddy's low voice faded in and out.

"Wouldn't you rather I destroy her pictures than kill the
little brat?" came JoAnne's response.

I never really knew what particular crime of mine had
brought about that storm. Now I suspect that JoAnne's rages
were fired as much by her problems with Daddy and his drinking as by anything we girls did. But at the time it seemed to us
that anything could set her off.

Invariably, these outbursts would spur JoAnne to extrava-
gant expressions of remorse, never made directly but jotted in
little notes that she'd leave us in our rooms. Then I'd feel
constrained to forgive her, no matter how much hurt and resentment I was still feeling over her bruising words and actions.
During the worst blowups I would sometimes take a bottle of

JoAnne's drugs and lock myself in the garage, though I could never bring myself to actually take any pills. Then I'd berate myself for getting cold feet. Not only did I live in constant fear and humiliation, but I was also a coward.

That summer my Dad's kids from his first marriage came to visit for a week. JoAnne tolerated them, all the while jibing at Dad about all his kids and ex-wives, but I could tell that the pressure was really getting to her. By the end of their visit, she had given him an ultimatum. "It's Angie or me," she demanded. "You choose."

Unwilling to learn his choice, I gave Dad an out by asking my half-sister, Gloria, if I could come to Indiana with her family. She agreed and we made the drive back, stopping at the Grand Canyon along the way. But the ride was anything but a pleasure trip. Not only was I teased mercilessly by Gloria's two young sons, but her mother, my dad's first wife, was traveling with us. I was profoundly relieved when we pulled into Indianapolis one week later, just as the sun was coming up over the horizon. Feeling awkward about staying at Gloria's, I just rested on her couch until it was a decent hour to wake Grandma and Grandpa Carver, who lived just up the street. That afternoon, my cousins—the four daughters of my mom's twin sister— came over to welcome me, and we excitedly cooked up plans for me to move in with them.

My aunt was divorced and worked nights as a cocktail waitress, so we girls came and went as we pleased. JoAnne had kept me on tenterhooks, desperately afraid of doing something wrong, but now I had no supervision whatever and I was overwhelmed by my new freedom. One wild night I was introduced to cigarettes, alcohol, and drugs all in one fell swoop.

I spent that summer bouncing between my various relatives' houses and, toward the end, went out to see Dad's family farm. My grandmother was in a rest home, and so the house had been unoccupied for years. Tall weeds and grass smothered the little cracked steps where I had trotted along with Carrie and Chris. The paint of the little house was cracked and peeling, and the screen door balanced on one hinge. Behind the house stood a lone cement wall, tarnished with black soot, starkly out of place amid the tall grass and ringed by pieces of splintered wood. It was all that remained of the old red barn that had been so alive in my imagination. Staring at the ruins, I silently wished that I would just disappear like Carrie, Uncle Sam, and the barn. I just couldn't go back to life with JoAnne.

But I had to return. I was home only a day before the tension threatened to engulf us all. So I was packed off to stay with my cousin Melanie for a week until I could move in with her oldest brother Taylor and his wife, who lived nearby. There I enrolled in school and again got swept up by the dizzying freedom that was the flip side of JoAnne's stifling supervision. My cousin let me drink and smoke—they even bought me cigarettes—and allowed me to smoke marijuana, though only at home. It wasn't long before I was skipping school and doing hard drugs with my new friends.

Just before Christmas break I skipped out one morning with a friend who had procured some PCP that we did together. When we went back to school that afternoon, I stopped in the bathroom, where I stood in front of the mirror for an hour talking to a "new student"—my own reflection. When the bell rang, I couldn't find the bathroom door, and when I did, it wouldn't open. Panicking, I decided that the school day had ended and that the janitor had locked me in, and I started to scream until another student rescued me. She showed me that I had been pushing on the door, when what I needed to do was pull!

The next morning Taylor told me that I had been expelled from school and that my dad was coming to get me. Now all the emotions I had been crowding out with drugs and alcohol surged up in me. I missed my dad and Toni so much that I wanted desperately to go home. I even missed the order that JoAnne imposed on my life, as much as I dreaded her rages. But I was sure that she would never have me back.

When Daddy arrived, I confessed about the drinking and the drugs—everything that I had gotten mixed up in. Then I started to cry. "Oh Daddy, now where will I live?"

He hugged me tight and called me his little sweetheart. He wasn't angry—he even told me how sorry he was that things had gotten so bad for me. And he delivered the words I most longed to hear: "I'm taking you home," he said.

FIVE

I don't know how Dad worked things out with JoAnne, but when I got home, she made a real attempt to treat me with respect. It seemed that all of us had made a new commitment to be a family, and so that Christmas and the first few months of the new year were more peaceful than at any time in our life together. JoAnne had started going to church again, taking Toni and her daughter, Cindy, with her. I joined them, just to be conciliatory at first, but I grew to love my church like a second home. Its members were so genuine, so life-loving, and they showed me such kindness and acceptance. Through them, I was nourished by a newfound faith in God. It was during this time that JoAnne told me that she'd learned what it was she had been sent back to life to do. Her mission was to bring me to God. I knew that she was right.

And so it came as a devastating blow when Jo-

Anne broke down again. It happened on a beautiful spring Sunday. JoAnne had missed church for a few weeks, and Toni and I would attend with another family. We were sitting on a pew near the front of the chapel when a man came down the aisle and handed me a note. It read, *Your father called. You need to go home immediately.*

As we pulled up to the house, I felt sick when I saw the ambulance with the flashing lights on top. Please let Dad be all right, I prayed. Darting inside, I could hear JoAnne crying and fighting with the paramedics. I stood at the top of the stairs as two large men took her out to the ambulance. My stomach was churning and I struggled to breathe as JoAnne sobbed apologies, but this time anger overrode my fear. At first her dramatic suicide attempts had left me consumed with fear and guilt, but now I secretly wished she would just do it and get it over with. I hated her for what she put us all through every time she swallowed a bottle of pills.

By then my mother was also living in California, and we would visit her a couple of times a year. With JoAnne gone to the hospital, Toni and I moved in with her for a week. I arrived with my suitcase, my pillow, and a blanket in case my mother didn't have a real place for us to sleep. Then as I bounced around her new apartment—I'd never seen it before—I spotted my old red blanket spread across her bed. How I'd missed it! I dove into its warmth. I hollered out to my mother, "Can I trade blankets with you?"

Mom stopped in the doorway. "What did you say?" she asked.

"Don't you remember? This is my old blanket. I gave it to you when you left for Bear Creek," I said.

"You did?" she asked.

"Yeah!" I reminded her. "I said you could have it because I didn't need it anymore."

"I don't remember, honey, but you can have it back," she said.

Immediately I clutched it to me. I was relieved to find that it still had its comfort-giving magic, which I needed more than ever.

Later, when Mom asked about things at home, I griped about JoAnne's control. "She won't let us go anywhere, and she's mad all the time," I said. When the subject of school grades came up, I confessed that for as many A's as I received, I got the same number of D's and F's.

"Well, you really *are* a screwup, aren't you, Ang!" she observed with her usual careless bluntness.

Her words stung, though I knew she didn't mean to hurt me. We saw too little of each other to allow for such reproaches. I got enough of those at home. Although I hadn't quite grasped the powerful link between the two, I knew that my inability to concentrate in school had begun when my mother left home. If I was a screwup, she had contributed, and I suspect that she sensed that truth. I think she also sensed my discomfort with her world. We were too much like strangers for her even to recognize how deep my problems ran. When the week was over, Toni and I were back with Daddy.

There were a few more suicide attempts, and then JoAnne decided to leave my dad. They were divorced when I was seventeen. The stomach attacks that I always got when JoAnne was angry persisted even after she left. One day when I was at the movies with some friends, my stomach started to burn. I had grown accustomed to the pain of these attacks, but I could tell that this was going to be a bad one. After a few miserable minutes, I whispered to the other girls, "You guys, I have to go home. I'm sorry."

"Are you okay?" asked the friend next to me. I went weak as the fire in my stomach climbed up my throat. Frightened, she insisted on escorting me home. All I could say was "Hurry," as I held back the tears.

By the time I got there, I was in a cold sweat and my temperature was skyrocketing. Terrified, Dad took me to the hospital.

When the nurse explained that she was going to pump my stomach, I panicked. Daddy calmed me down and watched nervously as the nurses shoved thick surgical tubing up my nose, back down my throat, and then into my stomach. The whole procedure took several hours, and he spoke encouraging words to me throughout it, assuring me that the torment was almost over. By then it was very late, and he had to go home.

"No! Please don't leave me," I begged.

"I have to go to work in a few hours, honey," he gently said.

I was afraid to swallow or to move, and so I lay awake the rest of the night, praying silently. A day later, despite my high fever, my gallbladder was removed. "You had enough gallstones to build a house," the doctor joked.

I was released a week later, but I didn't recover. I was vomiting constantly and running a fever of 104, so again I was admitted to the hospital. None of the tests revealed a clue as to what was wrong with me, and I grew more sick and frail with each passing day. Then the days stretched into weeks. Daddy had brought me my red blanket, which was a tremendous comfort. My mother called and sent flowers once, but she never came to see me.

My second family, my friends and church members, rallied to my side. Their cards and flowers streamed in, and my room was packed with company every minute of visiting hours. I had so many visitors that the hospital finally propped an easel in the lobby with my name and room number on it to spare the staff the onslaught of requests. Then, on my eighteenth birthday, I was wheeled out into the lobby. As I was pushed through the double doors, I was greeted with balloons and streamers and a rousing chorus of "Happy Birthday" from my friends. What a wonderful surprise! I had never imagined that so many people cared about me.

But my condition kept worsening. At night I slept fitfully, and I frequently had incoherent dreams. I could barely walk and only with help. One day I pushed the button to call a nurse to take me to the rest room. Nobody came, and so I attempted the trek on my own, supporting my eighty-five-pound frame on the portable monitor that held my IV. It took me several minutes to get across the room, and then my IV monitor started beeping, the sign that it needed to be plugged into a socket. I squatted down to insert the plug and then found myself too weak to stand up. I couldn't even summon the strength to yell for help. All I could do was sit and cry until my roommate woke up and rescued me.

I had test after test, with no clear diagnosis. The doctors knew that my life was in serious danger, and I had begun to despair. One night when my minister came to visit me, his face went pale when he saw my state. He told me that the congregation was holding a special fast and offering prayers for me. When he left, I felt comforted enough to be able to sleep peacefully for the first time in many nights.

By the next morning, the incision from my surgery had

ballooned out so that it looked like I had a little puppy in my abdomen, stuffed underneath the scar. When the nurse saw it, she rushed out to call my doctor, who dashed in wearing his three-piece suit, accompanied by a team of nurses armed with surgical instruments. The nurses held and reassured me as the doctor cut open my sutures again. I had developed an abscess that was polluting my body and killing me. When my incision was reopened, the poison could escape, and finally my recovery began.

The doctors thought I was lucky that the abscess had emerged in time for them to check the infection's spread, but I believed that more than luck had intervened. The love of all my friends, who cheered me and pushed me to get well; and the faith in God of my fellow church members, who prayed and fasted for me—that is what saved my life.

SIX

There was one member of my church family who was coming to dominate my thoughts. His name was Richard, and from the moment I met him, I knew I'd found the kind of man I wanted to marry—strong-willed, decisive, and in control. Like me, Richard had had a difficult childhood. His parents were divorced when he was nine, and his mother had raised her children alone. The family was destitute. Richard remembers days when he only got one meal—the free "government" lunch at school—and being ridiculed by other students for being poor and for not having a father. And like me, he'd learned to cope with his family problems by turning to God.

Being intelligent and determined, he'd gotten into college, and while that made me proud, I couldn't imagine life without him. So I hopped a Greyhound bus to visit him in the Rockies. It was our first real date. On my second visit he gave me an engagement ring that his best friend had made by hand. It was a little chipped, but I cherished it. We were so desperately, ecstatically in love that I abandoned California for a rented room across from his apartment so I could see him every day. We were married four months later.

Richard had secured a job as a research assistant for the university. With real paychecks in our future, we could use our meager savings as the down payment on a little Datsun that Richard's brother was selling. The weekend before Richard's job started, we took the car down to Southern California for an extended test drive and a visit to my family. We drove all night without stopping except for gas.

We arrived tired but too excited to sleep, so we decided to rest up on the beach for a few hours. We laid out our towels in a nice spot, and Richard put the car key in a little pocket inside his swimming trunks. We spent the afternoon body surfing and sleeping in the sun, enjoying our first minivacation together as a couple. When the sun began to fade, we packed to head back to Daddy's house. Richard reached into his pocket for the car key. "Oh, no!" he shouted. "It's gone!"

"You're kidding!" I said.

"No, I'm not kidding!" he hollered. "How can I get back for my job on Monday?"

All our money—forty dollars—was locked inside the car.

"Calm down," I said. "We'll find it." I started sifting sand through my fingers.

We scoured the beach until Richard plopped down in the sand, in frustration. "This is completely pointless," he fumed.

It's a measure of how central religion was to our lives at that point that I suggested, "Richard, let's pray."

"Oh, yeah," he said. "And the key will miraculously appear."

"Come on, let's just try it."

Kneeling on the deserted beach, we quietly asked God to help us get home in time for Richard's new job. But no, the key didn't miraculously appear.

There was a rental shack up the beach, where a scragglylooking teenager let us use the phone to call my dad and every friend I could think of. Nobody was home. Finally, I called a locksmith who wouldn't come unless we paid him $76 in cash. By now the sun was setting, and the boy who ran the rental shack was getting eager to close up. Explaining our dilemma, we begged him to stay open a little longer till we could figure something out. He thought for a minute or two and then said, "Listen, I have some money. I was going to use it to get high tonight, but you guys are in real trouble. So just take it, and send me a check when you get back to school."

We were so touched that he would trust us that much. "See," I whispered to Richard. "I guess we did get a miracle." We gratefully accepted the offer, and of course kept our promise to pay the kid back.

Not long after the "miracle" on the beach, Richard and I were married. I was so excited to be moving on into my own life. I had dreamed of the day when I would have my own family, my own home, and my own children to love; and especially a husband who would love me in return. In the beginning Richard's love completely filled me up, crowding out all my anxieties and fears. The other things that had sustained me—my friends, my church family, the comforts of religion—seemed like pale and ineffectual substitutes for the security of marriage. Richard, I thought, was all I needed.

That's not to say that I knew how to be a wife. We were both just kids and had no idea how to handle the pressures of fusing two lives into one. That was clear from the night we moved into our first apartment. While we were unpacking, Richard came across a sheaf of my unpaid bills. "What are these?" he demanded.

"Well," I said, "that's my old phone bill, and that's—"

"How could you just run up a bill and not pay it!" Richard interrupted.

"I was planning on paying them. I just forgot," I replied, a little sheepishly.

"Fine, fine. I'll pay them," he said, half disgusted.

And so a pattern was established in our lives. I made mistakes and Richard fixed them, but not without a lecture.

We'd been married for only a few weeks when Richard's aunt Francine approached him about sending her ten-year-old son to live with us. She was having marital problems, and Richard had always been close to Jimmy. We were discussing the prospect, but then one afternoon while Richard was at school, I got a phone call. It was a woman with a thick southern drawl, and I figured she must be my mother-in-law. Everyone in Richard's family had such heavy southern accents that I could never understand them.

"Er ya'll riddy furra veezater?" said the voice.

"I'm sorry, can you say that again?" I asked, a little embarrassed.

She repeated the question, "Er ya'll riddy furra veezater?"

I just couldn't ask her again to repeat the question so I said, "Uh, okay." Two weeks later, Jimmy arrived on our doorstep.

I suppose I can be forgiven for resenting him. Here I was, a new bride, just starting to build a life with my husband of less than two months, when my privacy was completely destroyed. Jimmy and I clashed bitterly. But worse than the loss of privacy was the tension that permeated our new home as Jimmy continually tested me. I felt that he deliberately did things wrong to make me angry, and I was jealous of his bond with Richard. Stuck between two warring parties, Richard grew withdrawn, sometimes staying at the library to avoid my rants about Jimmy —what a mess he'd made of the house or about how he'd embarrassed me by telling a snoopy, imperious neighbor that Richard was going to "fix me" for telling him what to do. Richard's withdrawal, of course, made both Jimmy and me more anxious, and our clashes grew more frequent and more bitter. I hated feeling abandoned by Richard; I hated the constant turmoil; and worst of all, I hated the recognition that I was sounding like JoAnne.

Jimmy lived with us for a year and a half. By the time he moved back in with his mother, I had a whole new view of JoAnne's behavior. She'd made my life miserable for six long years, but now I could see how much she'd sacrificed for me and what she'd been trying to teach me. I was grateful for the tremendous gift she had given me, my reintroduction to God. Still, it scared me to find such a deep reservoir of anger within myself, and I was desperately afraid that my reactions proved that I shared her illness.

My fears abated somewhat with the birth of my son Alex. In caring for him, I found the patience and love that had eluded me in dealing with Jimmy. Maybe I wasn't the perfect wife or stepmother, but when I held my son for the first time, I dedicated myself to being everything he could possibly need. And I was, for a while.

Jimmy's departure didn't magically heal the breaches that

had developed in our marriage. Money remained a problem, especially when tuition had to be paid. I'd contributed to our support by waitressing and baby-sitting as well as sewing—I was an accomplished seamstress and even established a small clientele. When Alex was born, I got a job as a telephone solicitor, working at home, so I could take care of him. I became adept at feeding him and even changing his diapers while talking on the phone.

Alex had been born during final exam week of Richard's last semester in college. Even so, Richard graduated with honors in psychology. During his last push before graduation and while he hunted for a job, I took charge of our finances. When things got really tight, I would charge groceries at a nearby gas station/convenience store or float checks to get by.

One day Richard caught on to my money-stretching tricks. Alex had a persistent rash from his cloth diapers, which I'd been washing by hand because I didn't have the money for the laundromat, and so I bought some disposable ones with a rubber check. I planned to cover the check in a day or two when I got paid, though I knew Richard would hate my messing with his credit rating.

Unfortunately, Richard picked up the mail that brought the notice of the bounced check. It made him furious.

"Not only did you bounce a check, but we'll have to pay a ten-dollar fee!" he shouted. "How could you do something so irresponsible?"

"Irresponsible! I'm the one with a job," I protested.

"Yeah, right," he said. "If we could live on the kind of jobs you get, I could have ten job offers to choose from by this afternoon. But I have an aversion to wearing paper hats."

"Hey, at least I bring home a paycheck."

Shaking the bank notice in my face, Richard smacked me in the forehead with it.

"But you can't live within our income," he countered. "I'm not your dad. It's not my job to always bail you out."

"Well, if I hadn't wasted the last three years putting you through school, cleaning your stupid house, and taking care of the baby—"

Richard interrupted, "Putting *me* through school? Until six months ago I was working two jobs and going to school full-time. And who stopped you from going to school? It's not my fault that you got D's and F's in high school. You seem to be fulfilling your intellectual potential right now, Miss Telephone Sales Expert, and if you don't go to jail for writing hot checks, the sky is pretty much the limit for you, babe."

Bursting into tears, I stormed out of the room. How dare Richard imply that I was stupid and a failure? Still sobbing, I pulled a suitcase from the bedroom closet, threw it on the bed, and started shoveling in my clothes.

Richard followed me. "What are you doing?" he asked.

"Well, I sure wouldn't want to be a burden to you," I told him, my teeth clenched in rage.

"Oh, so now you're leaving. This is just like you, you and your mother. You always leave someone else holding the bag," Richard said.

I was over the edge now, consumed with fury. "At least my mother didn't marry a jerk like I did!" I screamed back. "For your information, that check was for diapers; Alex needed diapers. If you spent more time changing diapers and less time watching TV, you might know that." I grabbed his bootleg videotape of *Star Wars*. "This video probably cost more than that bag of diapers. And I suppose you had to have it." Still crying, I broke open the protective guard and yanked at the tape inside until it snapped. "Here! This is what I think of you and your videotape and your college degree!" I hurled the tape into the fireplace, where a small fire was still smoldering.

Richard stared at me icily. Then he snatched a pair of shorts that I had designed and made for myself. "If that's how you want it, fine!" he said, tossing my shorts into the fireplace.

I rescued my shorts, but they were on fire. I stomped on them to put out the flames, but it was too late. They were destroyed.

"How could you do that, Richard?" I sobbed.

"You're right. I think it's counterproductive to be destroying our own things, don't you?" he said.

"I hate you!" I raged, heading for the living room, where I grabbed the tiny wooden shoes that I had toddled around the house in as a child, until I could no longer squeeze my little feet into them. They were the only vestige of happiness from my childhood. "You want to hurt me, let me help you." I tossed the little shoes into the flames. Forcing myself to watch them burn, I was seized with regret but when I saw Richard's face, I got a spark of gratification. Now he'd have to take me seriously. He'd know how unhappy I was. . . .

Indeed, he looked genuinely shocked by what I'd done. Then he started to laugh in horror. "You're crazy," he said.

"You're crazy!" I screamed back.

"No, really, I think you're certifiable. You shouldn't be allowed to walk around loose," Richard said.

"I hate you!" I was howling as I snatched our framed marriage certificate from the wall. Realizing my intent, Richard leaped forward and tried to grasp my wrist. "Oh, no you don't," he said, but he was too late. I smashed it into the fireplace. As it burned, Richard grew solemn. "What is wrong with you?" he asked.

"I don't know. I'm sorry," I cried, moved by his concern and chagrined by my fever of destructiveness.

"I'm sorry too. Don't worry about the check. We'll work it out."

But the check was the least of my worries. I was horrified by the monster I was becoming.

SEVEN

fter graduation Richard accepted a commission in the
Air Force. For the first time in our marriage, our finan-
cial tensions eased up. But military life brought me
new anxieties, for Richard's future depended a great
deal on me. I had to assume my place in the pecking
order of wives on the base, curry favor with the
spouses of his supervisors, and conform perfectly to
certain standards of womanly behavior at all times—in
short, I had to fit in. Officers' wives who couldn't or
wouldn't measure up would cost their husbands pro-
motions. I felt that both Richard and I were on duty
twenty-four hours a day.

Our first duty assignment was in Florida, where
Richard spent all day at the base while Alex and I
sunned on the beautiful beach behind our apartment
house. I woke up to tropical breezes and the sound of
waves lapping the shore. My life looked idyllic, but I

was unraveling with the dual pressures of motherhood and my new social responsibilities. I was also tormented by dark memories that seemed to be working their way to the surface, memories of sexual abuse and the feelings of self-loathing they sparked in me. Between those obsessive thoughts and my periods of JoAnne-like rage, I felt that I was going crazy. What I would come to think of as "the cycle" was kicking in.

One afternoon Richard came home from the base and told me, "I found a nice little church down the road. I think we should go." By now I had grown so distant from spiritual things that I could hardly mention church or God anymore without feeling guilty. I hadn't prayed meaningfully in several years. So I changed the subject, but a few days later Richard brought it up again. "Come on, Ang," he said. "You haven't been to church in ages."

"Fine," I said, thinking I would come up with an excuse by the time Sunday came. But when I woke up on Sunday, Richard was already dressed in his suit and had Alex ready to go too. Obviously, Richard was not going to be put off.

The service seemed to bring all my confusion to a head. It was excruciating, for it seemed obvious to me that I no longer belonged here with these people—perhaps I never had. My mind flooded with the grim thoughts that plagued me all the time now. *Why had God let such horrible things happen to me? I must have created them. I am a useless person, a terrible wife, a mother possibly unequal to my son's "terrible twos."* I felt panicked and sick, flooded with the sense of contamination I'd felt when I was younger, back in the days of my eating disorders.

Richard didn't seem to take account of my distress. On the way home from church, he asked, "Well, how did you like it?"

I didn't answer. I could see the wheels turning in his head

already. This church attendance wouldn't be a one-time thing. He was planning a whole program. I was going to be his next project—I was to be reclaimed, redeemed. I knew Richard well enough to realize that he wouldn't let up. He would keep turning up the subtle psychological pressure until he got his way or he drove me crazy.

Sure enough, he asked, "Would you like to go again next week?"

I felt like screaming. Why couldn't Richard see what I had become, that I never was what I had pretended to be? I wanted to jump out of the car. I was so obviously beyond the reach of God that no amount of church was going to do me any good.

Then suddenly I knew what I had to do. "I want to go," I told him. But I didn't mean "go to church." I meant "go away."

The next day when Richard left for work, I packed everything I could fit into the car. Whatever I couldn't cram in, I left strewn around the apartment. I dropped a note to Richard on the table saying the minimum: *I'm leaving. It doesn't have to be permanent. It's not all your fault. . . .* Then I strapped Alex into his car seat. Maybe I was running away, as my mother had, but I wasn't abandoning my son.

I wound up in Southern California, where I worked nights as a waitress so I could be home while Alex was awake. Richard called nearly every day to beg me to come home. He was being reassigned to Tacoma, Washington, and he wanted me with him. He even sent me a pair of beautiful, expensive pearl earrings that I knew he couldn't afford. But I refused to be persuaded. I had a whole new life, going drinking with friends when my shift was over and finding that I liked the oblivion that alcohol could bring, associating with people who expected as little from me as I would get from them. . . . I was free of the suffocation of marriage. I had escaped.

Then one morning I woke up with a boozy headache, with the events of the night before completely blacked out. And I realized that I was still haunted by my dreams, and that my careless life in California was only fueling my sense of worthlessness. I was abusing my body and, worse, punishing my innocent son for my misery by depriving him of his father. And by keeping him from Alex, I was causing Richard pain. Nothing I was doing made sense.

And I set off for Tacoma and the new home I'd never seen, hoping to give marriage a second chance.

EIGHT

R ichard had always been kind and tender with Alex, and now he was bending over backward to be gentle with me as well. He didn't even flinch at the stack of unpaid bills that I had run up in California. He was so happy that I was finally home, and so was I. For a long time the only arguments we ever had were about my family. Richard still harbored some resentment toward my mother and Toni because he suspected that they had encouraged me to leave him. But to be fair, I have to admit that my family did little to heal the rift.

The ill will was almost palpable when we visited my mother in California. Toni and her boyfriend met us at Mom's house, so we could all drive to dinner together. Alex was tired and hungry, and as we worked our way through an impossible traffic jam, he threw a tantrum. We asked my mother to stop at any restaurant along the way, but she insisted on taking us to her special place, assuring us that it would be worth the wait. All week she'd seen me indulge Alex's every wish, so she didn't take his outburst seriously. Even when Alex grew uncontrollable, she told us to hang on just for a few more minutes. I felt like she was saying, "Since this is my treat, we are going to do it my way."

At last we arrived and ordered, but Alex kept fussing, prompting several stylish couples around us to stare and complain. Leaning over, Richard said, "Why don't you take him for a walk?" I jumped at the chance to be excused from the tension. In the best of times, Richard and my mother tolerated each other only for my benefit, and this dinner was growing unbearable.

Once we got outside, Alex calmed down. I walked him around the block for a while until my family filed out of the restaurant. "So how was dinner?" I asked Richard when I got him alone.

"Well, your mother took this opportunity to set me straight on proper parenting technique."

"Oh, really. Was it good advice?"

"It was loud advice."

"How loud?"

"Plenty loud, and with quite a few obscenities."

"Really?"

"Really. Your mom was explaining to me and the rest of the restaurant that we were giving in to Alex's whims. Then she said we were putting too much pressure on him with our unreasonably high expectations."

"I don't understand. Do you think we have exceptionally high expectations of Alex?"

"I think your mother was exceptionally high."

"I don't think she was high, I think she was a little drunk."

"Angie, please don't defend her. For the record, I think she was both, but that's neither here nor there. Being blitzed didn't change what she thought—it just gave her a convenient excuse to mouth off about what she's thought all along."

"Can you blame her for criticizing you? She knows that you hate her."

"I don't buy it."

"Don't buy what? You do hate her."

"I don't buy your whole argument. I reject your entire premise. I don't hate your mom, but even if I did, how would that entitle her to criticize us—loudly—in public? Not being liked may make her *want* to do it, but it doesn't *entitle* her to do it!"

"But still, if she—"

"Oh please, shut up. I mean it, shut up. It's bad enough to have to swallow parenting advice from the person who is quite possibly the single worst parent on the planet without having to hear her biggest victim come to her defense."

"I'm not her victim."

Richard was livid now. "You see yourself as the victim in every situation except this one, when you really *are* a victim. You don't see how you've let your whole worldview, your entire self-image be colored by your parents."

"What do you mean?"

"I mean that I feel like I pay for your mother's mistakes. You seem to have a complete inability to accept responsibility for your actions. She taught you that by her absence. If you don't like what I say or something is too tough to handle, you withdraw or find some other way to escape. If we have a heated discussion when we're driving somewhere, I have to worry that you'll jump out at the next red light. That's not normal. Every unlikable trait in your mother that I see mirrored in you scares me to death. Do you really think she . . . is she any kind of an example for you? Are you going to continue to do the things you've seen her do?"

"You don't know how much it hurts me when you talk so harshly about me and my family."

"Alex and I are your family too. When you act unstable, like we don't matter, like nothing matters; when you act like you might desert us when times get tough—we pay." Then, as suddenly as his tirade began, Richard stopped himself. "Well . . . I've gone too far haven't I? I'm sorry for the way I've said this."

I didn't say anything.

"Here, at least let me slow down to fifty-five miles an hour before you jump out this time."

I just stared out the window for the remainder of the drive. One thing that was too tough to handle was the possibility that he was right.

NINE

ow that Alex was almost two years old, I started thinking about having another baby. Toni had been my anchor during my childhood, and I wanted Alex to have the same security. I had loved being pregnant with Alex, and I yearned for that happiness again. I also thought that another child might strengthen my bond with Richard.

So we tried, but I didn't get pregnant. I had conceived Alex almost the minute we started planning, but now every month brought disappointment. As the year dragged on, the new truce I'd established with Richard grew fragile and strained. We started carping at each other again. Finally, my longing for a baby was so strong that I got down on my knees for the first time in years and pleaded with God to send me a baby. Jacob was born nine and a half months later.

Alex's birth had filled me with peace, but Jacob's

plunged me into depression. I felt so guilty for bringing a child into such an unstable marriage and so afraid that I wouldn't be able to cope with the pressures of a new baby. Richard and I fought bitterly for a while, but it was even more frightening when our arguments gave way to an angry silence. For long periods we would refuse to speak to each other unless it was absolutely necessary. Divorce seemed inevitable, but I was determined to hang on, to prove to Richard that I was not my mother. Even when we stopped speaking, I took care of the kids and the house, ironing Richard's uniforms and packing the sack lunches he took to work every day. For a while I even wrote little love notes and hid them in the bag or in his briefcase.

I made a half-hearted attempt to go to church with the boys. Richard was no longer interested in attending because that would mean committing himself to me and our marriage. I suspected that I was attending myself only to make a show of being a good wife. I still felt completely spiritually disconnected.

Then one day, when Jacob was four months old, I saw a TV news story that brought all my old torments into focus again. A child had survived an abduction and the most brutal sexual mutilation I'd ever heard about. Fired by pain and anger at my own sexual abuse, I called the TV news station and learned that a group of citizens was forming to fight for changes in the laws governing violent sexual offenders. I quickly grew completely immersed in the cause.

Richard objected to the long hours I spent organizing and attending protests, but he could see that I didn't care what he thought. I spent a year working with the group, dragging along my infant son and three-year-old or occasionally leaving them with baby-sitters. I took pride in my righteous work, but I wasn't prepared for the toll it would take on me. Hearing the stories of other victims of sexual abuse brought my own poisons to the surface. I started obsessing about the abuse again, unearthing new, horrible memories that were too big and too painful to accept. I felt powerless to defend myself against them. I started sleeping days and crying nights. I started drinking again, heavily. I knew I needed help, but I didn't know where to turn.

Finally, I went to see my minister, who was a kind, understanding man. Something inside told me to trust him, though I believed that my problems were way out of his league. I confided that Richard and I were hardly speaking anymore, that we had drifted so far apart that I feared nothing could save my marriage. Then he looked intently at me and said, "You're not putting notes in Richard's lunch anymore." I was stunned. I had been too embarrassed by the silly gesture ever to tell anyone about it, and I was sure Richard would never share such an intimate detail about our life. The minister continued, "You need to start doing that again. You don't know how much those notes affect him. They give him hope."

I told him that I could not face the anger and depression that engulfed me. He hesitated to counsel me, but I begged him, "Please. Just tell me what to do."

He stroked his forehead intently and then leaned forward in his chair. "If I tell you, then you must do it," he said.

"Of course I will," I replied through my tears.

"If you read the Scriptures and pray, then God will take care of the rest."

I couldn't believe that just reading and praying could heal me. But nothing else had helped, so I thought I better trust my minister's inspiration. He'd known about the notes in Richard's lunch bags, along with some other details of my life that I'd thought were pretty well hidden. Perhaps he was on target this time too.

But there always seemed to be some big obstacle to prayer. Every single time I knelt to pray or opened my Bible, the phone would ring, Jacob would cry, or Alex would pitch a fit. It was uncanny—it was almost as if some power were trying to keep me from following his advice. It wasn't long before I abandoned the effort altogether. I was no longer the naive girl who thought you could look to God when you lost your car keys, never mind when you thought you had lost your sanity.

Finally, inevitably, I packed to leave again. By now Richard seemed relieved, worn out by the emotional storms, the months of cold silence, and the uncertainty over whether I would stay. I got a job selling BMWs, which would give me a car as well as the income I'd need to live on, and until I could find an apartment, I spent nights with friends. I came home only during the day when Richard was at work.

That's where he surprised me. I was sitting on the kitchen floor sorting through some papers—the birth certificates and address books that I would need—when he walked in. The look of urgency in his eyes persuaded me at least to listen to him. "We need to stay together," he said.

"Yeah, right."

"No, really. I have the distinct impression . . . It was like I felt a voice come into my mind, telling me that we need to be together to raise the boys, Alex in particular," he said. "They need both of us. You are supposed to go see your minister. He will be expecting you."

Oh, good. Another ploy to keep me here, I thought. I

looked at Richard with disgust and started to pick myself up off the floor.

"Wait," he insisted. "You know I'm not the kind of weirdo who hears voices and crazy stuff like that," he went on. "I was told that this impression came to me because Alex has been praying for us. You won't have to take my word for it. You'll know for yourself."

"You're kidding" was all I said. I wasn't even sure that Alex knew how to pray, though he did go to Sunday school.

Hearing the acid in my voice, Richard shrugged and headed back out the door. Then he paused for a second, turning to look at me with an expression of tired resolve. "You know, Angie," he said, "ultimately, it's going to be up to you. I could go either way. I'm as tired of fighting with you as you are with me."

Richard left, and I shook my head in annoyance that he would try such an obvious manipulation. I finally had the guts to get out of my marriage, and nothing was going to stop me. But then, two days later, when I was out apartment-hunting, I stopped at a red light. I allowed my thoughts to wander back to Richard's insistent words. Then suddenly I felt a powerful burst of energy that began in my chest and spread throughout my body, filling me with an undeniable certainty that what Richard had told me was true—that he had received a message from God. The certainty was confirmed when I went to see my minister, who told me that he had been expecting me. He'd had a hunch that I needed to talk.

And so on the very eve of what was to be our final breakup, Richard and I made the commitment to stick together. A few weeks later came a sign—or so we thought—that we had made the right decision. Richard got a new assignment in Okinawa,

Japan—far away from our families, my political action group, and all the other triggers of trouble in our marriage. If there was anything we needed then, it was the chance to start over; and we'd been granted it.

TEN

kinawa is a jewel of the Pacific, a tropical paradise. When Richard was off duty, we loved to explore its caves and to snorkel in the jade-green water. Even the scary typhoons that would sweep over the island helped knit our little family together. We would spend hours, sometimes days, nestled together in our home as storms raged outside. My sons loved it when the typhoons knocked out our electrical power, so they could wander with flashlights through the darkened house, making ghost sounds that were all but drowned out by the howling wind and the deafening torrents of rain. Richard and I would snuggle up on the couch and watch the boys play for hours. When they were tired, we'd drape a sheet across the dining-room chairs and let them sleep in the homemade tent, while we stayed up yakking all night. In these relaxing times Richard's natural humor would bubble to the surface. Sometimes he would get me laughing so hard that I would cry.

Outside our window was a huge tree—or at least huge by Okinawa standards, in that it was big enough to climb. By the time we left Okinawa, it had been reduced to two slim sticks by the typhoons.

We quickly found a new community of friends at church who introduced us to the fascinations of the Japanese culture. A beautiful landscape, a new world to explore, warm genuine friends who made us feel that we belonged—our new life was absolutely perfect.

And so I was crushed when, right around Christmas, just like clockwork, I found myself in the grip of "the cycle." This time I was determined to beat it. I was coming to recognize that my depressions were seasonal, coming every January and June, and that they bore little connection to the events of my external life. Something inside me would open the floodgates of memory—of drunken holidays with Dad, of Mom's desertion, of JoAnne's furies, of my abuse—and with the memories would come the obsessive thoughts, the wash of self-hate. I would barricade myself indoors to sleep all day with alternative rock music playing on autorepeat. Even having to carry on a conversation could bring on an anxiety attack. But I thought that if I could weather the cycle this time, life would return to normal.

My best friend in Okinawa, Jennifer, would call, and I would make excuses to get off the phone. I couldn't even face going to the grocery store with her. But she persisted, refusing to take my rejection personally, realizing that something was making me perilously fragile. One afternoon she stopped by the house and, ignoring my protests, dragged me out into the sunshine. She simply would not allow me to disengage entirely from those around me.

Obviously, I needed help, but I was afraid to consult a psychologist on the base. The Air Force community was such a small world, and the last thing I wanted was for my problems to show up on Richard's service record. So I enrolled in an anonymous support group for survivors of sexual abuse. Again, hearing the other women's stories strengthened my tide of memories; and worse, it made me feel that my problems were impossibly grave. None of the other women had the cyclical disorders that I did; all that we had in common was a tendency toward anxiety. I felt like a freak, and that feeling was as frightening to me as my state of agony, and it made me fearful of confiding in anyone. Later I learned that my symptoms weren't so atypical, but they just didn't happen to be shared by the members of that little support group.

Now I told Richard that I needed a break. I wanted to go back to the States to see my family and to see if the depression would lift, but Richard was afraid that if I left again, I wouldn't come back. Still sure that my mom and Toni had helped me leave him the last time, he worried that, given my precarious state of mind, they might influence me again. So he refused to sign the paperwork that the military required for me to leave the island.

So I went through the motions of coping, dragging myself through the days, trying to deaden the destructive voices within me. One night when I went out to get milk at the convenience store on the base, I couldn't even bring myself to get dressed. I just slogged out of the house in my slippers and a pair of sweats. But when I got home, I couldn't make myself go in the house. I thought that if I did, I would explode.

So backing out of the parking lot, I drove until I found a place to hole up for the night. The next day I bought some clothes and toiletries, then washed my hair, brushed my teeth, and dressed in the store bathroom. I was moving in a fever of obsession. Unsure of what to do or where to go, I bought a ticket for the movies. The film was *Flatliners,* a story about death and a pretty apt reflection of my internal state. When it ended, all I could do was wander until darkness fell. Then I had no choice but to go home.

When I got there, Richard and the boys were in a panic, praying that I would come home. My heart broke at my sons' relief. Alex bounded to his feet, crying, "Mama's home," his eyes swollen with weeping. He ran to me and clutched my legs, refusing to let go. Richard jumped up to hug me, saying, "Are you all right?" in a trembling voice. Jacob, my toddler, stretched out his arms, crying for my embrace. "Mama, Mama," he called to me.

What evil impulse had made me hurt them? I couldn't believe I had been so cruel. Before, I had always announced my departures, but my leaving them for a night and a day without a word, without so much as a hint that I was alive, was so deeply unsettling that I had shaken their innocent trust to the core. My poor children—I feared that I had damaged them in a way that would lie dormant until, finally, when they had children of their own, it would emerge, too powerful, too massive to harness, and so they, too, would be consigned, as was I, to a dark, torturous existence. I couldn't control my urge to flee, and I could see, suddenly, its tremendous potential for harm.

"Where did you go?" Richard was asking me, without castigation or anger. This man loved me so much, but he didn't understand how sick and how angry I was. "I'm so glad you're home," he said, tears welling up in his eyes.

But what could I say to him? That I had spent twenty-four

hours shopping and seeing a movie? All I could do was choke out, "I don't know."

The next morning, the repercussions of my cruelty persisted. Jacob woke up early and insisted that I hold him all day. He clung to my neck as I made breakfast, balancing him on my hip. Alex, being older, woke up angry. As I bent to kiss him, he shoved me and retreated into the corner, where he crouched into a little fuming bundle. He masked his face with his hands and peered at me through his fingers. How could I convince him that I hadn't meant to shatter him? How could I know that I would never do it again?

At my survivors meeting that night, we talked about how important it was to delve deeply into our painful memories. I was reading a self-help book that corroborated our approach, counseling me to confront every detail of my childhood nightmares. But I couldn't—my psyche just wasn't ready to carry that burden—so I was overwhelmed with feelings of helplessness and failure. If the only way to overcome my past was to face it head-on, then I was doomed.

Understanding that my depressions were cyclical didn't help me withstand it either. Instead, the recognition made me see the future as a long string of destructive periods when I would wound everyone I loved. How could my husband and children accept the fact that these bouts were uncontrollable? How could they not hate me if I slipped into these states over and over again? And how could I, myself, stand having the misery return, year in and year out, for the rest of my life?

Such a future would be unbearable, impossible. And now I felt myself pass into a deep, profound, black abyss of despair. I saw myself as dead in every sense that really mattered—unable to enjoy the many blessings of my life, to love my husband and children without causing them pain, to move forward in life, surrendering the past. I had seen that leaving Richard was not the answer when I had "escaped" to Southern California. And finally a way out began to open, a vision of a more permanent escape. It was the only thing I could do to make things right, if only I had the courage.

ELEVEN

The morning of January 7 dawned clear and cool. I had been wrestling with my feelings for most of the night, finally drifting off to sleep on the couch only an hour or two before sunrise. I could hear Richard moving around upstairs, dressing for the early shift at work, then creeping down the steps as quietly as his combat boots would allow. He made his way into the living room, where I lay with my soft old red blanket crumpled beneath my feet. Pretending to be asleep, I tracked him through my eyelashes. I frequently watched him this way in the evenings and the mornings; his movements were sure and solid with such a comforting sense of purpose. I loved him so much. How long would it take for my craziness to exhaust his willingness to love me? If he did give up, even after enduring more than most husbands would, it would destroy him, I knew. He so keenly and clearly defined his own worth by how honorably he fulfilled his roles as father and husband. He was bending over me now, fumbling with the blanket at my feet. He pulled it up over my shoulders and tucked it in around me. Kissing me on the forehead, he whispered, "I love you."

When he left, I roused myself just long enough to pour some cereal for the boys, change the tapes on the stereo, and take the phone off the hook. Moving, even breathing brought an excruciating awareness that I was still alive and able to do damage. Hiding under my blanket for most of the day, I watched my boys play on the living-room floor. Their faces were so sweet. The thought that I had caused my sons suffering made my heart and stomach ache. This final act I was now contemplating would be a terrible shock to them, and though there had been so many signs along the way, it would be a shock to Richard too. I hoped that they would understand that my solution was an act of love, offering them all the chance for a happier life. Perhaps this was how my mother had felt, that leaving would save her children. I had become poisonous to everyone around me.

Richard brought home dinner that night, and pleading a touch of the flu, I stayed on the couch until he and the boys went upstairs. I could hear Richard moving fitfully about for hours, getting in and out of bed, pacing the floor. Finally, at two A.M. he came down the stairs and stood over me. "Are you coming to bed?" he asked.

"I don't feel good. I slept all day. I think I'll just lie down here awhile," I replied. His hesitant concern sharpened the tension between us. He knew that I was in trouble, and he wanted to make me come upstairs with him. But after my recent disappearing act, he was afraid to press the issue. "Go on, Richard," I told him. "I want to be alone."

He left, and I waited till the house fell silent to change the tapes in the stereo and sit down at the dining-room table. If I was going to execute this final act, I couldn't lose my resolve. It was all so unfair. I didn't want to leave my children, and I had wanted desperately to be a good mother. I cried bitterly, searching to imagine some way that I could stay with my family and keep their love. But I was convinced that my lingering would only cement their unhappiness. I had to set them free.

I picked up a pencil and my college-ruled notebook, spattering the pages with cold tears. Blackness had pried its way deep within me, paralyzing any goodness. I was so tired. Sick and tired. I started to write a farewell note: *I'm sorry, Richard,* I began. The tape clicked over on the stereo, hushed sounds that I realized I'd been hearing over and over. Hugging my old red blanket, I got up to change the tape. The soft, seductive lullaby hung in the air. I knew it well. The singer's lilting, sympathetic voice whispered affectionately of death. Oh yes, I thought, rock me to sleep. My voice joined his, blending harmony and purpose in our perfect duet of death.

Returning to the table, I sat half draped across it to finish my good-bye note. The tragic words I scrawled looked a little melodramatic, but so what? After hiding the shameful truth about myself for so long, I could finally stop pretending and accept who I really was, a person who was spiritually dead, embittered, used up.

Uncertainty stabbed me for a second as I thought again of Alex and Jacob, but then I gave myself over to the music. It caressed my weak and exhausted spirit, promising relief from my suffering. I drew the words and melody into my mind, breathing deep and full. My hesitation and fear were soothed by the sounds. I was ready.

Climbing the stairs, I called to mind the morbid tableau

that I had envisioned from time to time since Bear Creek. They would find my body lying in the tub amid swirling streams and clouds of blood. . . . The grotesque image of my own discarded body in my mind had brought instant satisfaction during the worst of JoAnne's assaults, and during the past few days, this picture of my death had been with me constantly.

I tiptoed into my bedroom to get the white cotton dress I'd left draped across the chair. It seemed so appropriate for this moment. Then I crept into the guest bathroom, locking the door behind me. With a pair of pliers, I crushed the casing around the safety razor to extract the blade, then I ran the bathwater and slipped on my white dress. As the tub filled, I stared at my face in the mirror. My eyes were black and empty. That made things easier—not seeing myself in my eyes. As I stepped into the warm water, I had a flash of triumph. Finally! It was time.

I cut along the veins in my wrists with the flimsy razor blade. It took ages even to draw a little blood, never mind the crimson spill that I had imagined. What a joke, I thought to myself, I couldn't even do this right. Pressing my bleeding wrists against my pretty cotton dress, I climbed out of the tub and headed downstairs, trailing water behind me. In the kitchen I rummaged through the drawers for a good knife, with no luck. I was such a lousy cook that the sharpest thing in my kitchen was the can opener.

Then I noticed a new prescription on the kitchen counter. In one frantic sweep, I swallowed the entire contents of the bottle. Blood was still running down my palms and dripping from my fingertips, but I was thrilled to have discovered the pills. They'd make it easier. While I waited for the drugs to work, I cleaned up the bloody mess I'd made of the kitchen floor, then went upstairs to drain the pink water from the bath-tub and to change into a robe. Wrapping my wrists with towels, I curled up with my blanket on Alex's empty bed. He had crept into our bedroom as usual. Now all I had to do was wait. . . .

Good, I thought, as I started feeling dizzy. Before long the room was flying around me, spinning like a carnival ride. I had a terrible thirst, and my body was slow and heavy as I stumbled heavily to the bathroom for a drink of water. Coming back, I was hit with a blast of nausea. I made it back to Jacob's room just in time to grab an Easter basket. How appropriate, I thought, grimly. Easter, the celebration of death and rebirth.

Since part of the prescription had come back up, I needed another dose of drugs. So, rummaging through the medicine cabinet, I created a more palatable and possibly more deadly concoction. This time I poisoned myself slowly, taking small but frequent doses throughout the early morning, so that my body wouldn't throw off the drugs.

At daybreak the sharp blare of the alarm clock from my bedroom was muted by the ringing in my ears. The shower started running, my signal to roll out of Alex's bed and crawl into my own. When Richard came out of the bathroom, he stopped and asked me, "What's the matter?"

"Nothing. I'm just sick," I slurred.

He accepted my explanation and left for work. When the boys woke up, I packed them off to a neighbor's house with a note asking her to watch them since I wasn't feeling well. Then I reestablished myself on the living-room couch, still clutching my blanket, the sweet friend of my childhood. I continued to dose myself with drugs, consuming as much as I could stand at a time without vomiting.

Finally, I got the sense that it was happening. I could no

longer stand or sit up. My eyes fell on the clock. It was eleven
A.M. A bright warm sun filtered through the thin drapes and
gleamed on the white tile beneath. That would be my last
glimpse of life, I thought. My nose and lips were numb, and it
was quickly spreading to my limp arms and legs. My tongue
was thick and dry as I tried to swallow. I felt myself going—
separating from my heavy, sluggish body.

TWELVE

I was passing over into a different sphere. I could feel a tremendous energy enfold me with a deep rumble, as if I were lying in the aisle of a Boeing 747 during takeoff. I lay motionless beneath my thin red blanket. My soul was disconnecting from my body with a hum that kept growing louder, rising to a whine as the vibration of death pulled me deeper. I could see what looked like the inside of my eyelids. Peachy-rose light softened the intense sinking, rushing sensation.

Morbid intrigue beckoned me to watch my death, so I lifted my heavy eyelids, and instantly I felt a huge surge of energy pull me back into my body. I could see the decorative pillows scattered around me on the couch. Shallow quick breaths and the thump of my heart told me that I wasn't quite there. Okay, I thought, I'll have to try again.

Closing my eyes, I wished for death. At once I saw

what I thought was the warm glow of morning light filtering through my eyelids, but this time I noticed there were bright red lines scrawled across the yellowish-peach background, weaving in and out, like dozens of tiny streets spread across a road map. At the same time I began to move through a cocoon of soft warmth toward a black spot at the end. I started to realize that I must be seeing some kind of mucous membrane, but it couldn't possibly be the inside of my eyelids. Instead my whole body felt enveloped in a warm, comforting embrace that gave me a greater sense of peace and security than I had ever experienced. Could this be death?

I still wanted to see myself, so again I opened my eyes, and again I was abruptly sucked back into my body, still lying in a crumpled heap on the couch. Now I knew that I was somehow controlling this transition between life and death. Though I had done what was physically necessary to die, I still had to choose.

Squeezing my eyes tightly, I engaged my thoughts and will toward death. I was pleased with myself, exuberant—I could hardly believe that I had the courage to do this thing. The trembling roar swallowed me up, and again I was sucked into the warm tunnel. Its golden walls, lined with blood vessels and capillaries, squeezed me as I passed through slowly. The experience felt familiar, though I knew I had longed to feel love like this all of my life.

Suddenly I felt the strain of contraction within my own abdomen. It was only later that I recognized what the strain meant, though I have borne two children of my own. I was experiencing my own birth, my first memory. My perspective was both that of a participant and that of an observer. I could feel the physical warmth and pressure from within the canal as well as my mother's contractions, just as she had experienced this joyous event twenty-seven years earlier. As if I were her, I could feel my mother's sense of awe, her reverence about what was taking place. I could feel my own excitement, my innocent love as a newborn baby entering the world for the very first time. There was no pain. I knew only the intoxicating euphoria of love, a wonderful tranquillity mingled with pleasant resolve. My mother wanted me, and I wanted to come to her.

Suddenly I was pushed out of the tunnel with great force and speed. Once outside, I could feel myself being cradled, my head resting in the calm support of a hand. I was gazing up at a woman, but since I could feel the emotions of both the woman and the baby, I wasn't sure which one of these people was me. From the baby's viewpoint, I didn't know who the young woman was, but I was secure in her presence. From the woman's viewpoint, I recognized the feeling that I'd had so many times as I held my boys, studying their delicate features with wonder as the cords of interdependency and security had solidified, creating the unique bond between mother and child. And as sort of an outside third party, I thought that this young woman must be me. She had my nose and my smile.

The woman was talking to someone I could not see, but the words sounded muffled and like nonsense to me. I was content just to be held, and I was not bothered that I couldn't understand what they were saying. I recognized that what I was hearing was a pleasant exchange, but that was all that the words meant to me. I didn't even expect to comprehend the adults' garbled talk. All I cared about was my intense feeling of peace and security.

Then the woman smiled down at me. I realized that her brown hair was straight, not wavy like mine, and shorter than my own. I recognized that this was my mother nearly three decades ago. I was enthralled with her and also part of her. I didn't seem at all aware of having my own body or my own life. I was aware of my very basic and pure feelings, but I had no sense at all of being an individual, separate and complete. I was tied to this woman who gave herself to me. She was my identity.

It would be a long time before I realized the significance of the fact that these first two memories—of my birth and of being cradled by my mother—were the most protracted, detailed, and emotionally colored of all that I would be shown. Through them I came to understand that my mother had cherished me just as much as I did my boys. I'd never imagined that—and so I could see her in a different way, realizing that what she'd done for us was the best she could.

My mother's attention was drawn away, and now I noticed that there was a large screen before me. I was being drawn into a three-dimensional slide show of my life that played out before my eyes chronologically, while I experienced every part of it from all points of view and all points of understanding. I knew exactly how each person felt who had ever interacted with me. In particular, however, I was being shown in vivid detail exactly what my childhood was really like. The pictures flew past me, but I easily absorbed every moment, each one triggering an entire memory or a chunk of my life. So this was what people meant when they said, "My life flashed before my eyes."

As each picture flashed before me, it filled me and I became immersed in it. In front of me was a birthday cake set on a spanking white Formica tabletop. Gold and silver glitter sparkled through the slick finish and brought a flood of memories of meals I had eaten in this kitchen. I could smell the sharp burn of candles as they stood proudly upon the cake, announcing that my fifth birthday had arrived. I was excited and fidgety. My crisp dress shifted as I moved, and I could sense its color— red. My feet, clad in little white socks and shiny black shoes, dangled over the edge of the cold chair, and the backs of my skinny little legs stuck to the vinyl seat. Wiggling around, I pulled myself up so that my legs peeled off the chair. The scene seemed so familiar and so real, but I felt that I had never experienced it before. I didn't know what was going to happen next, nor could I change the events.

I was sitting at the head of the table, surrounded by all my neighborhood friends. Birthday plates and plastic forks were neatly arranged. My next-door neighbor and best friend, Mary, seemed so mature, being two years older than me. Her blond curls bounced on her shoulders as she turned her head to look at the other children decked out in party hats. We were buzzing with excitement over these hats, strapped under our chins with thin elastic, and we were giggling and pointing at each other. These were things and people that I had completely forgotten.

Standing across the table from me, my mother was all-knowing, all-loving in my mind. Her slender form, so perfect, so beautiful, moved with elegant adult grace as she laughed and chatted with Mary's mom. Her arms were neatly folded now, but I knew she could perform any task flawlessly. Her bright smile testified to me that this was an important day and that I was the center of it all.

She interrupted her conversation to gently direct me in the next step, according to proper birthday etiquette. "Make a wish, Ang." The voices of happy children danced in the air. The mothers' shoes clicked and scuffled across the sparkling white tile as their attentive, commanding forms responded to the needs of squirmy partygoers. The cake was so magnificent, so huge, the candles on top all aflame. My job—to blow them out—was so important.

I could see my friends' faces so clearly that I felt I could touch them. Mary's sister, Susie, sat with her elbows on the table, her fingers propped against her lower lip. Her shyness apparent, she patiently waited for her piece of the cake while the other children called dibs on their little sections. Since it was my birthday, I was granted the honor of first choice and first piece. I felt so important. I was having so much fun. I was tiny and quick, full of energy.

Suddenly we were sitting in a circle in the living room. Like a silent ghost peering in, undetected, I could see myself squabbling with my little sister, Toni, over who was going to sit where. I wanted to have my favorite friends near me, and since it was my birthday, I didn't think that Toni should be allowed any choice in the matter. The outburst was quickly resolved. I watched in amazement as the grown-ups talked and the children became engrossed in the unwrapping of presents.

In front of the window stood the flocked, artificial Christmas tree that my dad pulled out every year. For a moment I thought that I had skipped to a later memory, but then it dawned on me that my birthday comes in early January and we must have left the tree up well past Christmas. Red, green, and yellow glass balls dangled from its fluffy white limbs. I was enchanted that each globe held a reflection of my face in its own color. The lower branches of the tree had a few silver cellophane needles exposed. Toni and I loved to crawl under the tree and pinch off the flocking, which felt so wonderful between our fingers. My mother was very upset when we did it, but the feeling was so satisfying that we couldn't resist.

Our new tract home was simple and immaculate. The big picture window that framed the Christmas tree let the Arizona sun paint everything with a white glow. Beloved and familiar objects came into focus: the scratchy green carpet, the beige vinyl sofa, my Raggedy Ann, of course, my red blanket, thick, new, and bright in this picture. My fuzzy blanket went everywhere with me. I loved it so much that I would pick the little "fuzzies" off and eat them because it wasn't enough to be wrapped in my blanket—I wanted it to be part of me.

I was living my childhood all over again, literally from everyone's point of view, including that of my adult self. As the somewhat callous third-party outsider, I saw that while all our furniture was new—the pumpkin-orange chairs with the thin legs and the plain cherry coffee table with rounded edges and narrow trimwork—it was unmistakably of the sixties. Simplicity and functionality rather than glamour were the decorating principles in our home. Above our large sofa was an elaborate gold-framed picture of stormy waves crashing on a rocky beach. It hung slightly off center.

But at the same time I was seeing it all through my eyes as a little girl, hatching detailed plans for playing make-believe and hiding in the forbidden drapes. The coffee table was a ballroom dance floor for my dolls, and the stuffed chairs were Barbie mansions, complete with rooftop decks. Shoes were doll cars. It was a world of magic possibilities.

From the outside I saw myself unwrapping a present. At the same time I was inside my own tiny frame, feeling the paper tearing as I ripped to see what was inside. It was an Etch-A-Sketch, and it seemed so big and awkward as I wrestled it out of the huge sheets of paper. Pure delight! I wanted to open all the presents as fast as I could. I was surprised by how little effort it took to scramble around and by how quickly my attention shifted.

Time sped past me again, and suddenly I was sitting on the kitchen counter making toast. It was a cloudy morning, but the sky was bright white. Soft light soothed and warmed the sharp lines of the toaster and the edges of the counter. My mother was there at the kitchen sink rinsing something off. I could hear the water swish and ping against the sink. I thought about the washcloth that was draped over the faucet. It was "yucky," and I hated having my face wiped with it. My mother's hands glided from the running water to the towel, and I admired the ease with which she accomplished her chores in the kitchen. She was perfect, and I was proud to be her daughter.

She was singing, as usual. Her gentle voice comforted and protected, but the song was an old familiar folk tune that was sad and created in me an uneasiness, feelings of foreboding. I wanted to cry.

It was another hot day now. The sliding-glass door was open, and I could hear a lawn mower humming in someone's back yard. Daddy was reading the newspaper on what my sister and I called the "kitchen couch," which stood against the wall in the dining portion of the room. I loved the word *davenport*, and sometimes we referred to the couch that way. We sat there to watch television. Daddy's legs were crossed, and there was a lit cigarette between his pursed lips. His head was tilted back slightly as the stream of smoke curled through the air. He was patient and adoring as he tolerated my energetic company. I was bouncing from his lap to the pine-green canvas cushions and then back on top of him. The skin on his face felt loose and sandpapery to me as I pressed my little hands against his cheeks. I loved to be close to him. The kitchen couch was thin and uncomfortable, and the cushion was easily shoved from its place with my foot.

Amazing! "Remembering" from my firsthand child's point of view was such a revelation to me. As an adult, I had retained only simple scattered memories from my childhood. But as my life continued to progress in hologram style, I was beginning to understand that I had forgotten very important emotions and events of my past. As a little girl, I had felt secure in my home and in myself. I saw myself with pure, accepting eyes. My emotions were clear and intense, not muddled and conflicted. My picture of myself was dipped in the pride and love of doting parents—the exact opposite of what I had come to believe. My mother's presence, especially, brought me warmth and happiness. She was the central figure in most of the early memories.

As my darker years approached, the images became less detailed. They had the same electrical charge, but I passed through them very quickly with confusion and detachment rather than with the full absorption and the emotional glow of my earlier memories. I was seeing single frames of my life from different time periods, with some events apparently being more significant than others because I went through them slowly. Many parts of my adult life—the parts I'd made peace with either by granting or receiving forgiveness—were brushed over or completely missing, though I knew that I could recall or refer to them if I wanted to. I wasn't permitted to stay in any of the later memories, so it seemed that this part of my life wasn't being screened for my own benefit. And indeed, I became aware that I wasn't viewing my life alone.

There was definitely a presence with me, though I could see no one. I knew that the presence was male and that he didn't judge my life—no condemnation or empathy emanated from him. The only feeling I got was, "This is the way it is. This is the life that you lived."

The closer I came to the end of my life, the faster the pictures flew past me. It was incredible! In an instant I had experienced the entirety of the twenty-seven years from my birth until the moment that I found myself dying on the couch and passing into the warm tunnel. Then the fast motion of my life rushing past and through me stopped abruptly.

Now what?

THIRTEEN

JoAnne had described death to me as an embrace, a warm enveloping of peace, but there was no peace in my deliverance. She had told me of the brilliant white light that surrounded her and of the familiar beings who welcomed her. The comforts of those reunions and the sense of being bathed in the glory of God's love—His light—left her and many others, I've since learned, loath to slip back into their old, comparatively empty and grim human lives. But for me there was no blaze of radiance, no arms waiting to usher me into the Divine presence. There was only blackness, as though I were suspended in outer space, unbroken by a single glimmering star.

I considered the possibility that my grandparents and my Uncle Sam had gone to Hell and weren't allowed to meet me, but I knew that my cousin Carrie couldn't possibly be in such an awful place. Surely her gentleness, her acceptance of her brief afflicted life, would have earned her a place in God's presence. So I peered into the dense blackness, willing her form to emerge. I looked in vain.

Where was I? I was immersed in darkness. My eyes seemed to adjust, and I could see clearly even though there was no light. I was aware that I was standing on what felt like solid ground, but nothing was there. The darkness continued in all directions and seemed to have no end, but it wasn't just blackness, it was an endless void, an absence of light. I knew that it had its own life and purpose. It was completely enveloping.

I was still very excited that I'd made it this far. Death was quite an adventure. I swung my head around to explore the thick blackness and saw, to my right, standing shoulder to shoulder, a handful of others. They were all teenagers. "Oh, we must be the suicides." With a laugh, I opened my mouth, but before I could form the words, they came tumbling out. I wasn't sure whether I had thought the words or had attempted to say them, but they were audible without my having to move my lips. Then I wasn't sure if these other people had heard me, until the guy next to me responded.

He had a tall, slender build and wild black hair that looked unnatural, as if he had colored it. He wore heavy black eyeliner. His appearance struck me as odd because I assumed that makeup and hair dye were physical things that a spirit would leave behind with his physical body. He was dressed in black, as were the others. His black T-shirt, rolled up to expose his upper arms, the leather vest, black denim jeans, and biker boots made me think that we shared the same taste in music. He didn't say a word to me. He slowly looked down at me and turned forward again. There was absolutely no expression on his face, no warmth or intelligence in his eyes. Suspended in darkness, he and all the others stood fixed in a thoughtless stupor.

Second over from the other end of the line was a girl who looked to be in her late teens. Her blond hair hung straight and dull about her narrow shoulders. I got the feeling that we were the only females in the group. I was coming to see that feeling —what some call intuition or the sixth sense—was the preferred method of transferring information here, where unvoiced ideas grew audible. As I exercised my new power of "sensing/ feeling," I had an inkling that I was remembering a long-forgotten, natural, familiar skill that had been supplanted or subverted by words, and I quickly grew proficient at this new way of gaining knowledge. I felt a fleeting hint of sadness for the blond girl, knowing how sensitive teenagers are and how overwhelming problems appear to be during those difficult years. Whatever made her kill herself was probably temporary and solvable. Nothing in her brief life could possibly have been so bad as to warrant suicide.

But she did not connect with me. Her empty gaze, fixed on nothing, continued uninterrupted by my thoughts about her. She was just like the rest of them, staring blankly forward, with no concern or curiosity about where we were. They were dead, and so was I.

Then came a *whoosh!* Suddenly, as if we had been waiting for a kind of sorting process to take place, I was sucked further into the darkness by an unseen and undefined power, leaving the teenagers behind. I was flying upright, moving at warp speed, like a comet shooting out of nowhere. I sensed that I was going faster than any man-made aircraft could fly, but without the physical effects of flight or the pull of gravity. Nor did I have any sense of the temperature, of the coldness you'd expect to find in deep space, or any way to judge time. I was probably flying for only a fraction of a second.

But how far had I flown? It could have been a long way—many thousands of miles, perhaps, or just the length of a football field—but I could not gauge it. I had no awareness of inertia, no sensation of slowing down as I neared the landing place, which I didn't see until I was upon it. In the final split second before my feet touched down, I got only a lightning glimpse of my destination—of crowds, of what looked like thousands upon thousands of other people massed below.

I landed on the edge of a shadowy plane, suspended in the darkness, extending to the limits of my sight. Its floor was firm but shrouded in black mist, swirling around my feet, that also formed the thick, waist-high barrier that held me prisoner. The place was charged with a crackling energy that sparked me into hyperalertness, a state of hair-trigger sensitivity. Again, I perceived my surroundings not through physical sensations but through a kind of telepathic intuition. The foglike mist had mass—it seemed to be formed of molecules of intense darkness —and it could be handled and shaped. It had life, this darkness, some kind of intelligence that was purely negative, even evil. It sucked at me, pulling me to react and then swallowing my reaction into fear and dread. In my life I had suffered pain and despair so great that I could barely function, but the twisting anguish of this disconnection was beyond my capacity to conceive.

What was this place?

I knew that I was in a state of Hell, but this was not the typical "fire and brimstone" Hell that I had learned about as a young child. The word *Purgatory* rose, whispered, into my mind.

There were a few pieces of simple furniture scattered about. An Early American vanity with an oval mirror stood to my right. Its finish was dark in color but worn with time, and it had two small drawers that were closed on each side. Strangely, without opening them, I could see that the drawers were empty. Behind me was a shellacked wooden chair, with its seat and back bolted to a heavy metal frame and legs, like the chairs I had sat on in elementary school. The chair seemed to fade in and out, almost like a ghost that was always present but only partially visible. I wasn't sure whether my ability to see the chair was controlled by the chair or by my own effort. I sensed that the molecular makeup of everything around me—the furniture and the ground—was thinner than the things of the earth, so that here things seemed less solid though they were far more real, indestructible. Everything was placed here for a definite purpose. The chair, I felt, was unrelated to my situation, but the vanity had definitely been put there for me. It was not until years later that I recognized its significance.

Men and women of all ages, but no children, were standing or squatting or wandering about on the plane. Some were mumbling to themselves. All whom I saw seemed Caucasian, but there was a visible darkness about them that wasn't an exterior element, like skin color. The darkness emanated from deep within and radiated from them in an aura I could feel. They were completely self-absorbed, every one of them too caught up in his or her own misery to engage in any mental or emotional exchange. They had the ability to connect with one another, but they were incapacitated by the darkness.

I gradually became aware of the sounds of a kaleidoscopic flurry of voices, and I realized that in this realm thoughts were the mode of communication. Around me I could hear the buzz of thoughts, as if I were in a crowded movie theater with lights down low, picking up the sounds of hushed exchanges. It was difficult to distinguish many complete thoughts, but one woman's in particular stood out. Middle-aged, with a bouffant hairdo, she was justifying herself, over and over again, as if she were speaking to the ghosts of her past, trying to fix blame. It seemed to me that she had been there for years, reciting the same dull, pointless words that none of us cared to hear. I got the definite impression that she had committed suicide.

I sensed that I wasn't entirely female anymore. I was the same individual that I had been before—my morbid sense of humor, my curiosity, my personality, the way I thought and felt remained, and my awareness of being female was also with me —but my form had been somehow reduced, made not smaller but less complicated. I thought that if I were to look down, I would have found that I no longer had breasts. The diminishing of gender seemed to apply to the others around me as well.

Everyone I saw was wearing dirty white robes. Some people's were heavily soiled, while others' just appeared dingy with a few stains. I am not sure what I was wearing. I sensed that the housecoat I had on when I lay down to die had been replaced by dark clothing, possibly a familiar black sweater that I had worn often that winter. It had become almost a badge of my depression.

Sitting next to me was a man who appeared to be about sixty years old. His hair was gray, and somehow I knew that his eyes were blue, even though everything here appeared in black and various shades of gray. This man's eyes were totally without comprehension. Pathetically squatting on the ground, draped in filthy white robes, he wasn't radiating anything, not even self-pity. I felt that he had absorbed everything there was to know here and had chosen to stop thinking. He was completely drained, just waiting. I knew that his soul had been rotting here forever.

Suddenly I realized that adherence to the code of time, attention to clocks and the effort to keep them synchronized, is something that seemed to be confined to the rigid earth world. In this dark prison a day might as well be a thousand days or a thousand years. It struck me that throughout the civilized world, we know to the second what time it is in any given spot on the earth, and yet we allow people to starve to death when we have the means to prevent such suffering. How strange that we care so much about time.

I was sure that this man, like the middle-aged woman, had killed himself. His clothing suggested that he might have walked the earth during Jesus Christ's earthly ministry. I wondered if he was Judas Iscariot, who had betrayed the Savior and then hung himself. The feeling that I might be standing next to Judas Iscariot was my own idea and did not come from the man. I felt that I should be embarrassed that I was thinking these things in his presence, where he could "hear" me. Even in the midst of being completely wrapped up in my own problems in life, I had always been considerate of others' feelings. But now I didn't care. I felt no desire to be helpful or even polite to him or to anyone else.

As my mind reached for more information, I felt tremendous disappointment. I seemed to be using all of my brain capacity. I could feel and completely know about everything around me just by posing a question in my mind or by looking in any direction. The possibilities for learning were endless, but I had no books, no television, no love, no privacy, no sleep, no friends, no light, no growth, no happiness, and no relief—no knowledge to gain and no way to use it.

But worse was my growing sense of complete aloneness.

Even hearing the brunt of someone's anger, however unpleasant, is a form of tangible connection. But in this empty world, where no connections could be made, the solitude was terrifying.

I missed my children and I wanted to run home, but I could see only futility in such thoughts. The darkness had claimed me, and I was rapidly becoming like the others here. And I was going to be here for an incomprehensible length of time. This was the place where hope came to die.

FOURTEEN

T hen I heard a voice of awesome power, not loud but crashing over me like a booming wave of sound; a voice that encompassed such ferocious anger that with one word it could destroy the universe, and that also encompassed such potent and unwavering love that, like the sun, it could coax life from the earth. I cowered at its force and at its excruciating words: "Is this what you really want?" The great voice emanated from a pinpoint of light that swelled with each thunderous word until it hung like a radiant sun just beyond the black wall of mist that formed my prison. Though far more brilliant than the sun, the light soothed my eyes with its deep and pure white luminescence. I sensed that the light could not (or perhaps would not—I wasn't sure) cross the barrier into the darkness. And I knew with complete certainty that I was in the presence of God.

Now within the brilliance I could see the form of a man draped in billowing robes of breathtaking whiteness. Pearlescent, magnificent hair flowed back onto His shoulders from a noble, rounded widow's peak. He was a being of light, not just radiating light or illuminated from within, but He almost seemed to be made of the light. It was a light that had substance and dimension, the most beautiful, glorious substance that I have ever beheld.

From the light I felt love directed toward me as an individual, and I was baffled by it. I had never felt deserving of God's love. Anytime I had an inkling that He had taken a hand in my life, I felt that I had probably benefited as a casual bystander because someone else in my life, someone better, someone more deserving, had received God's blessings; so a little of God's love had accidentally spilled over onto me. I had been taught that God loves all of His children and all of His creations. Naturally, I categorized God's creations and assumed that we each get our little parcel. But having ranked myself with the trees and fish in importance among God's creations, I now saw that I had limited my ability to feel His presence and concern for me. I had grossly underestimated my importance and the nature of my origin—I am literally the spirit offspring of God.

I even looked like Him. I was surprised that He really had a body with arms and legs and features like mine, and I immediately fixated on His nose. There was a bump on the bridge that tapered into a sharp point, like a nose you might find on a Greek vase painting. An unusual characteristic of mine is that I, too, have a bump on the bridge of my nose, which I inherited from my mother. As I studied the features of God, I marveled to see that what I had learned in church and from the Scriptures, which I had assumed was figurative or symbolic, was apparently literally true. We are actually, physically created in His image. This realization was staggering.

Probably because of the brilliance of the light, which was white, God looked to me like an old man without wrinkles and with a young, strong body. His shoulders were broad, and His chest was full. His arms were strong, and the muscles well defined. His chiseled facial structure was strong and perfect, softened by a great white beard. But more striking to me than His physical features was the light that emanated from them. All beauty, all love, all goodness were contained in the light that poured forth from this Being.

I have since caught glimpses of this light in the splendor of nature, and I have felt portions of this intense light in people who love without judgment and who give without pretense. Occasionally I have felt the presence of spirits of light, and it is this kind of light that comes from them. But there is nothing that we are even capable of imagining that comes close to the magnitude of perfect love that this Being poured into me. I was captivated by His beauty. Yet as much as God filled me with wonder and awe, I was certain that I was not meeting Him for the first time. There was a tremendous familiarity about Him. While I was not remembering *details* of a life before my mortal birth, I was reacquainting myself with the life that I shared with the Father, a spirit life that seemed to extend to the beginning of the universe.

I could see that none of the others in the plane were aware of God's presence. The man cowering next to me could see that I was focused on something, but it was apparent that he couldn't see anything beyond the barrier. Others continued to babble unaware.

Then God spoke to me. His words were excruciating: "Is this what you really want?"

Of course, I didn't want to be separated from my family and from the people who loved me, but I had no choice. I was a failure at everything that was important to me, and I had tried to change the course of my life with disastrous results. I was sure that it wasn't a matter of what I wanted but of what I was capable. I could not succeed and I could not stand the pain of defeat any longer. I felt that this dark place was where I belonged.

Now His voice exploded with energy. "Don't you know that this is the worst thing you could have done?" I could feel His anger and frustration, both because I'd thrown in the towel and because I had cut myself off from Him and from His guidance. I stood there with the same stone face that I had worn as a teenager as I endured lectures by JoAnne over my poor grades, which she and my dad warned me would severely limit my options in later years. At the time I had almost no concept of life after high school, and I suppose a little of that attitude had followed me into adulthood. Certainly I'd had no real concept of suffering the consequences for my actions after I died.

And I'd felt trapped. I had been able to see no other choice but to die before I could do any more damage in life. So I answered, "But my life is so hard—"

My thoughts were communicated so fast that they weren't even completed before I absorbed His response: "You think that was hard? It is nothing compared to what awaits you if you take your life."

When the Father spoke, each of His words exploded into a complex of meanings, like fireworks, tiny balls of light that erupted into a billion bits of information, filling me with streams of vivid truth and pure understanding. "Life's sup-posed to be hard. You can't skip over parts. We have all done it. You must earn what you receive."

Suddenly I felt another presence with us, the same pres-ence that had been with me when I first crossed over into death and who had reviewed my life with me. I recognized that He had been with us the whole time, but that I was only now becoming able to perceive Him. Then I'd sensed His powerful, yet gentle personality, but now I could feel Him so strongly that I could even ascertain His shape. What I could see was bits of light coming through the darkness, like tiny laser beams pinpricking a black sheet or like stars peeping through the blackness of a cloudless night. Some stars are stronger than others and some are barely perceptible, and in the same way some of the specks of light penetrating the darkness were not entirely visible to me. I had to exert real effort in order to see them. This light was unmistakably of the same brilliance as the glorious light that emanated from the Father, but my spiritual eyes were incapable of fully beholding it. My ability to see with my eyes was somehow linked to my willingness to believe.

The rays of light penetrated me with incredible force, with the power of an all-consuming love. This love was as pure and potent as the Father's, but it had an entirely new dimension of pure compassion, of complete and perfect empathy. I felt that He not only understood my life and my pains exactly, as if He had actually lived my life, but that He knew everything about how to guide me through it; how my different choices could produce either more bitterness or new growth. Having thought all my life that no one could possibly understand what I had been through, I was now aware that there was one other person who truly did.

Through this empathy ran a deep vein of sorrow. He ached, He truly grieved for the pain I had endured, but even more for my failure to seek His comfort. His greatest desire was to help me. He mourned my blindness as a mother would mourn a dead child. Suddenly I knew that I was in the presence of the Redeemer of the world.

He spoke to me through the veil of darkness, "Don't you understand? I have done this for you." As I was flooded with His love and with the actual pain that He bore for me, my spiritual eyes were opened. In that moment I began to see just exactly what it was that the Savior had done, how He had sacrificed for me. He showed me; He had taken me into himself, subsumed my life in His, embracing my experiences, my sufferings, as His own. And so for a second I was within His body, able to see things from His point of view and to experience His self-awareness. He let me in so I could see for myself how He had taken on my burdens and how much love He bore me.

And I knew where I had gone wrong. I had doubted His existence. I had questioned the authenticity of the Scriptures because what they claimed seemed too good to be true. I had hoped that there was truth to the idea of a Savior who had given His life for me, but I had been afraid to really believe. To believe without seeing requires a great deal of trust. My trust had been violated so many times in my life that I had very little to spare. And so I had clung to my pain so tightly that I was willing to end my life rather than unburden myself and act on the chance that a Savior existed. He wanted to comfort me and to hold me, but we were separated by my responses to the lessons of life. He had been there for me all through my life, but I had not trusted Him.

Now I understood the Savior's complete understanding of me and of how the events of my life had unfolded to create so much suffering. Not only did I feel that He knew my life and my pain exactly, as if He had actually lived my life, but He understood everything about me. He knew how to guide me through the treacherous course. He knew my future, and He knew how my different choices could produce either more bitterness or growth, depending upon my willingness, my desire. Having thought all my life that no one could possibly understand what I had been through, I now knew that there was one other person who truly understood. His love surrounded me, melting me, and flushing out all residual feelings of worthlessness.

As I watched from the Savior's perspective, His unique comprehension of my predicament was transferred to the Father. From my new perspective I saw God in profile as He was looking at my form. The Father and His Son's communication was so rapid, so perfect, that they seemed to think each other's thoughts in unison. Jesus was "pleading my case." There was no conflict or argument here; Jesus' understanding was accepted without dispute because He had all the facts. He was the perfect judge. He knew precisely where I stood in relation to my need for mercy and the universe's need for justice. Now I could see that all the suffering in my mortal life would be temporary, and that it was actually for my good. Our sufferings on earth need not be futile. Out of the most tragic of circumstances springs human growth.

This place, this Purgatory, this Hell-like state, had a different kind of suffering—pointless, redundant, and stifling. This was the agony—useless, never-ending torment—that awaited me for taking my own life. But still I did not see how I could have saved myself from the driving current of events that shaped me, leading me to the point of despair where suicide was the only answer.

The Father interrupted my thoughts. "I told you how to get through this." And I flashed back to my minister's office and to the advice he had made me promise in advance to obey: "If you read the Scriptures and pray . . ."

Like a fool who unknowingly stashes a priceless Renoir in the attic with basic garage-sale fare, I had ignored the key to life that was gathering dust on my bookshelf. Powerful truths are contained in Scripture, and because I didn't understand or believe them in their entirety, I had dismissed them. I regarded the Scriptures as cryptic messages intended for the spiritually elect who are given the special privilege of understanding them. And many times I limited my own understanding because I felt that the messages in the Bible were contradictory or outdated. I couldn't see how they had any bearing on the problems of my life.

Feeling deserted by God and undeserving of guidance, I turned inward, tearing at myself, looking for the way out. I cut myself off from the world. My conversations with people never reflected my true feelings. I was self-contained and didn't allow anyone into my inner world. All of my emotional energy went to surviving, to staying afloat, until I found that as each day passed, I had less and less of that energy, less and less of the will to live.

I could now see that prayer is the key to unlocking the truths that are contained in God's written Word. The Scriptures are the textbooks, but God is the teacher. Without His guidance much of His written truth is lost because it is subject to our interpretation. Of course, we are all students, and until the author of the work explains His symbolism, sometimes we just don't get it.

Having been stuck in a sensible, finite world where tangible proof outweighs the importance of "feeling" or "sensing," I had tried to mold everything into concrete images to fit into my comfort zone. But now I realized that I was capable of drawing strength from the Scriptures if I would just accept the power of their simplicity.

FIFTEEN

s God the Father and Jesus were teaching me, their words picked up speed and power and then merged, so that they were saying the exact same things in the very same moment. They shared one voice, one mind, and one purpose, and I was deluged with pure knowledge.

I learned that just as there are laws of nature, of physics and probability, there are laws of spirit. One of these spiritual laws is that a price of suffering must be paid for every act of harm. I was painfully aware of the suffering I had caused my family and other people because of my own weaknesses. But now I saw that by ending my life, I was destroying the web of connections of people on earth, possibly drastically altering the lives of millions, for all of us are inseparably linked, and the negative impact of one decision has the capacity to be felt throughout the world.

My children, certainly, would be gravely harmed by my suicide. I was given a glimpse of their future, not the events of their lives but rather energy, and the character that their lives would have. By abandoning my earthly responsibilities, I would influence my children, my oldest son in particular, to make choices that would lead him away from his divine purpose. Before Alex was born, I was told, he had agreed to perform specific tasks during his life on earth. His duty was not revealed to me, but I felt the energy that his life would have up until his young adult years. He was clearly to be given a role of pivotal consequence in the lives of many. I knew that most of the pain of my death would eat at him and pull him down, destroying all hope and good in him. Without me, he might well be rendered incapable of completing his assignments on earth.

My son Jacob's life was different because he was already performing a sacred errand for God. I was shown that I knew and loved him before I was ever born, and that he had chosen to come to earth as my son. He had taken a tremendous risk in coming to me. When I was pregnant with him, the security of my marriage had hung by a thread. Divorce seemed imminent, and I had been weighed down by guilt over how I had been living my life. I was an emotional wreck, and I felt that I was a horrible mother. One night, my despair was so great that I had carried a loaded shotgun out to the back yard and pressed it against my tonsils. I couldn't pull the trigger because of the life, Jacob, that was growing inside of me.

My mother-in-law's love and kindness were a great support to me during that time. She arrived on my due date on a special ticket that allowed her to stay for only one week. She was coming to help with the new baby and, unwittingly, to heal the rift between me and Richard. But since Richard was stuck working a rotating schedule, they had very little time to talk.

All week long I kept having contractions, but didn't go into true labor. Then while Richard was driving his mother to the airport, I got a wave of contractions so quick and hard that I could barely dial the telephone. Jacob was born thirty minutes later, while Richard and his mother were sitting in the airport terminal having their first meaningful conversation in ages. She was lovingly counseling him to stay with his family, to be patient with me. Had Jacob arrived any sooner, Richard—and I— would almost certainly not have had the benefit of her wisdom.

So Jacob came to me as a messenger of love. He came to give me a reason to stay balanced, however precariously, on the thin wire of life. He'd had the option to wait for me to mature or to choose another mother, but he had sacrificed security in order to help me. This is all that I was given about his life. I am not sure whether his life here is going to be short or if his later missions would have been jeopardized by my death, but I was allowed to glimpse only his childhood.

I was told that my children were great and powerful spirits and that up to this point in my life, I had not deserved them. I caught a glimpse of how deeply God loves my boys, and how with my callous disregard for their welfare, I was tampering with the sacred will of God.

Then I was shown how I would harm other people close to me, such as my husband and my sister, Toni, by taking my life; and by extension, countless others. There were people on the earth whom I would never meet who would be affected by my suicide. Because of the anger and pain I would cause them, my loved ones would be unable to store up the goodness that they were meant to pass on to others. I would be held responsible for the damages—or the lack of good—they would do while immersed in the pain of my selfish death. And I would pay dearly for it, since spiritual law dictates that all of the harm, including lack of good, stemming from my death be punished by a measure of suffering. Even though I couldn't foresee the ripple effect my death would cause, I would be held accountable. God Himself is bound by spiritual law, and so there could be no escape for me.

And I was shown that for me, the plane of darkness was quite literally spiritual "time-out," a place where I was supposed to grasp the gravity of my offenses and to pay the price. But I had to ask, why me? Why was it that I could see God while the vacant husk of a man next to me could not? Why was I absorbing light and being taught, while he was hunkering down in misery and darkness?

I was told that the reason is willingness. When I first looked at that man and wondered if he had been alive during the earthly ministry of Jesus, the question showed that I was *willing* to believe in God, willing to believe that Christ had once walked the earth. And once I was willing to believe, I was able to see. Willingness and ability are the same thing. All around me on the dark plane were people of varying degrees of willingness, of understanding, of ability to see that Jesus Christ was there with us the whole time. I don't know if the others were talking to God as I was or if they were talking to other messengers of light that I was not yet capable of seeing, but I'm sure that not all of them were just mumbling to themselves. And I could see that my spiritual "time-out" could have lasted a moment, or it could have taken me thousands of years to progress out of that dark prison, depending on when I reached the point of willingness to see the light.

And what about the spiritual law that required me to suffer for the damage I had already done in life, up until and including my suicide? I was told that the debt had already been paid, that the sacrifice had already been made. In the Garden of Gethsemane, Jesus Christ had experienced all the suffering that has or ever will take place in the life of any human born on this earth. He experienced my life, He bore my sins, He accepted my grief. But in order for the agony that Jesus endured on my behalf to count, in order for Him to take my place in fulfilling that spiritual law, I had to accept His gift.

My heart broke as I realized that I had been not only hurting my family, who are beloved children of God, but also causing my Savior, who had such all-encompassing love and compassion for me, to suffer—all because I had allowed myself to be molded by other people's weaknesses.

The way that others mold us was revealed to me in this way: Everything has procreative power, even the dandelions in my back yard. A single dandelion is hardly a threat, but if it's left too long, the tiny seeds will scatter. New weeds will sprout, which will scatter their seeds, and the cycle will continue. Contagious disease spreads in the same way; and this is the pattern that all things spiritual follow. Expressions of love that are nurtured will take root in the soul. They will grow and mature, producing new seeds that will scatter across the lives of those with whom we come in contact. And the cycle will continue.

Some seeds will die when they reach ground that is infertile. We are the groundskeepers, and we create soil that will be most suitable for whatever crop it is that we want to grow. Some of us are careful gardeners who pull out annoying and potentially dangerous weeds, leaving plenty of room for good things to grow, things that are intentionally planted and nurtured. Others of us are somewhat careless, not systematic enough about removing the bad and harvesting the good. Still others are poor cultivators, who create the perfect breeding ground for destructive weeds that crowd out all the desirable vegetation. I belonged to the last group.

I had wandered through life in a haze, picking up a little here and there. The philosophies that are preached on daytime talk shows, differing doctrines and differing opinions, were fertilizers that did me little good. I hadn't learned how to sort the good from the harmful, and so the reality that I had accepted as truth was so muddled that the good was unrecognizable. The soil of my garden was inhospitable for healthy plants. Worse yet, I had methodically pulled any sprouts that were good, and I had fed the weeds.

One weed I tended, for example, had grown from the seed of my stepmother's unhappiness. She was cursed with migraine headaches as well as a multitude of emotional problems that were the result of a painful childhood. She expected us children to be on our very best behavior at all times. One day when I was home sick from school, I tried to turn on the television, which had been rolled into my room to keep me occupied in bed. Nothing happened. I went to my stepmother, who insisted that I had broken it, and while her words have worn with time, I still can feel her negative energy. When she was through chastising me, I went into the kitchen to make some toast, and as my stepsister passed me the loaf of bread, I dropped it. What with my illness, the stress of the scolding, and my fear of being in trouble for wasting a loaf of bread, I just blacked out, crashing into the wall and smashing a ceramic planter with my head.

Was my stepmother's anger unjust? Yes. But when I gradually embraced that dark energy I was nurturing a noxious weed.

The soil that my weeds loved was tainted by the untruth that I had accepted about myself—that I had somehow asked to be hurt. I had protected abusers all my life and felt that I was a co-conspirator because of it. In this soil all my negative thoughts about myself were free to bloom and to overrun my garden. I had allowed them to crowd out most of the light within me.

Before I took my life, I had come to an emotional crisis that forced me to look at myself honestly. After intense scrutiny I came to the conclusion that others, not me, were responsible for their hurtful actions; that I had not brought them upon myself. So I had corrected one deficiency in my soil, but I didn't complete the process to see that by this logic, I am responsible for all of the pain I have caused others. And so anger toward the faded enemies of my past germinated and created a whole new crop of lies. All the negative feelings I had embraced—hatred, self-pity, selfishness, all the rest—had grown up around me, their vines twisting, strangling me and encroaching on everyone around me, especially the people that I spent the most time with, my children.

I saw clear evidence of this encroachment during the time I was separated from Richard. I was living in Southern California, working nights as a waitress. I would swap baby-sitting with a friend who worked days and who was also separated from her husband. I would pick up her boys when I got off work in the morning, watch them along with Alex all day, then deliver all four boys to her in the evening. It was a great arrangement. One afternoon, I took all the kids to a drive-in restaurant, and my son was throwing one of his usual fits. Alex was nearly two then, and I attributed his constant outbursts to his age. But one of my friend's sons asked, "Why is he acting like that?" I replied, "Oh, it's just the stage he's in. He always acts like this." The boy said, "Oh no, not at our house."

Clearly, my son had been reacting to his surroundings. He

had been picking up anxiety from me and from the irresponsible life I had been leading. He had become entangled in my vines.

Sorrow fell upon me as I reflected on the time and opportunities I had wasted and the lives I had affected. I could now see that we create the soil, the state of mind that will allow us to tap into the nurturing power of the Spirit of God, the light, or we cultivate a personal atmosphere that stifles good and encourages darkness. I was now coming to understand the properties of darkness and of light.

SIXTEEN

S cience, of course, recognizes that all color is contained in light, including colors at each end of the spectrum that are not visible to the naked eye. Just as the rainbow is only a narrow segment of visible light, so too the light we see with our physical eyes is merely a thin band of the broad spectrum of light that exists. There are colors unimaginable and depth unmeasured within the full breadth of light, God's light. Light is multidimensional, and so is darkness.

Light is the essence of all that is good—beauty, pure love, truth, knowledge, sacrifice, concern for others, and so on. Wickedness, perversions, depravity, hatred, and apathy, impulses that strike us to hurt one another, the lies we tell, the hurtful words we throw like daggers—all are aspects of darkness. Darkness is not merely the absence of light. It is the energy of which evil is made.

With my spiritual eyes I could readily see that darkness and light are literally tangible elements and that everything in creation has a spirit side that is filled with either darkness or light. As I stood there in the darkness before God and His Son, I could see clearly how these two beings had their own bodies, their own spirits, how they were separate and how at the same time they were so completely one. It was the light that united them. Their individuality came from having separate bodies and separate spirits, but the light that was their most extraordinary attribute was the same. The light has fluidity and can be transmitted by using thought energy; and so can darkness.

We too have three facets. The fact that we all have bodies is obvious, and from the moment at my Uncle Sam's funeral when I saw a dead body for the first time, I knew without question that we have a spirit that occupies our bodies for a time and then leaves. But body and spirit are only two of the elements that make up a whole being. The third is an essence of darkness or of light. Most of us have a combination of the two, and the proportions of each shift with each thought that is conceived in our minds, with every television show that we watch, with the words that we say, and with each of our interactions with other people. Even a smile can alter the balance. We have incredible power to create for good or for evil by the substance—light or darkness—that we use to form our words and deeds and even our thoughts. A thought, whether it is composed of darkness or of light, is literally a deed in embryo. While many thoughts are aborted, all actions were first thoughts. A thought given voice is empowered and has a staggering ability to hurt or heal. Through words of light, through thoughts and crushing acts of darkness, we forge our own and others' destinies.

Being mortals, we see the world through mortal eyes that cannot detect the light or darkness in each other and in ourselves. Through our physical senses we can perceive certain elements of darkness and of light, but those elements are only a small portion of the whole. It is through our spirit that we can increase our ability to recognize broader bands of light and of darkness. Love, for example, is an element of light that we perceive through feeling. We don't see it with our physical eyes or handle it with our physical hands, but we know that it exists. Love is an energy that we can read through our spirits. All of our emotions have an essence made up of some level of light or darkness.

Just as physical darkness inhibits our ability to see, if we are filled with darkness, we become spiritually blind. When enough darkness gathers, it is so invading, so thick, that it is nearly impossible to see or to feel light. It is so much easier to absorb light when there is already light in us. And like the bands of light that we perceive with our physical eyes that can illuminate our physical surroundings, there are invisible wavelengths of light that can reveal things to us that we do not see in such obvious ways. If we don't have a certain amount of light in us, we cannot recognize darkness. This is why, for example, I could feel the negative energy behind JoAnne's actions, but not recognize the impact of my own.

I was told that everything is either good or evil. There is no gray area or in-between stage. Light is light and darkness is darkness; and like oil and water, darkness and light repel each other. Sometimes the two are tightly intertwined and it is difficult to see them separately, but they never occupy the same space. That is why God could not come into the darkness of my prison but remained just outside the misty boundary. That is also why I could not leave the darkness. I was filled with darkness, and my spirit was incapable of occupying space that was filled with light.

The same principle applies within us. There is no such thing as being a passive observer. Everything that we should have done but neglected to do has an impact. Darkness or evil is drawn to itself. Light and all that it encompasses is drawn to light.

Now I recognized these effects in my own life. While many of the impressions that I had about myself had originated as the painful words and hurtful deeds of others directed toward me, I had also been given messages of good about myself from my parents. I also had good feelings about myself that came from my friends and from fellow members of my church who took an interest in me, and from the thoughts and deeds of light I was able to create, especially during my teenage years.

There is one particular moment of light that I remember from that time. My stepmother's grandmother—Grandma B, we called her—lived in a nursing home. My family would visit her periodically. My sister and I dreaded those visits, hated the smells of urine and old people and hated being shoved up face to face with death. But one Christmas when we were visiting Grandma B, Toni and I decided to wander around. We were struck by how many lonely old men and women there were, slumped over in wheelchairs lining the corridors, with no one to visit them on Christmas. Having some musical talent and having nothing better to do, we decided to sing Christmas carols for the five or six patients who were in the main gathering area. Before too long, the room was filled with people, many of them singing along with happy, crackling voices. I felt peace and happiness so great that afternoon that I didn't want to leave.

That day we chose to create light. It is a fact that when a spiritual law is broken, there is a consequence. The same is true for the good we create. There must be an increase in light in us when we cultivate deeds that are positive, when we serve others voluntarily, with no thought of gain for ourselves. Sometimes we perform acts of service to others for the world to behold. While our motives don't diminish the good deed, when we seek the honor of mankind for our sacrifices, the rewards we gain balance out our sacrifices, and there is no increase in light.

My actions that day helped create light in me. My ability to create it taught me that I had the choice at any given time to create a new reality. I didn't have to allow my stepmother's anger or my abusers' selfishness to ravage my garden. I'm not saying that I could have completely escaped damage, but Jesus was with me through every tormenting act of injustice that was forced upon me, just as He is with each of us, living with us through the bad and the good. God certainly does not intend for His children to be abused, especially those who cannot protect themselves. But it is possible for the abused to come to forgive rather than be destroyed by others. It is difficult, but it is possible. I could have enlisted His aid in the struggle.

I just didn't know it then. What is the difference between a person who has no power to direct his life and a person who has the power and doesn't know it? None.

And not knowing, I let the darkness build up in me. I could see how my harsh judgment and accusations of others in my life had limited my own ability to progress beyond blind hatred. We tend to help victims of abuse and loathe the offender, dismissing the fact that he was once a victim. Yet it's impossible to know another's pain or to judge even the slightest offense unless we have also lived that person's life and know how every moment has affected that individual. With the same misguided logic, we tend to help others only when we think that they are helpless. Consequently, many of us refuse to offer a hand to those who we think are capable of providing for themselves but instead wander our streets in rags, with all of their worldly possessions in a bag or shopping cart. But each life is significant. It is neither our responsibility nor our right to pass judgment on each other.

Our destiny is then determined by our conscience, our ability or willingness to absorb light. Unless we choose to accept a finite level of darkness, we have the ability to grow forever. We decide.

SEVENTEEN

s my understanding was awakened, the light that nourished me made all things clear. As I was soaking in the
magnificent light, I was being immersed in pure
knowledge, pure love—all that is good. And in the
immersion many truths were revealed to me.

I understood that everything that enters our
minds influences us and can alter the balance of light
and darkness within us. Around the time of my death,
I had found myself attracted to morbid and dark litera-
ture as well as television and movies of a dark nature. I
watched a nighttime serial religiously that centered on
the murder of a teenage girl in a small town. The dia-
logue was a hodgepodge of nonsense and deeply symbolic teachings that were of the darkest essence. The
show was quite the craze, and "followers" often
quoted from its script, discussing the possibility of hidden meanings. I did, too, and so increased the measure

of darkness in my spirit. At that time, almost all my clothes were black, a seemingly insignificant coincidence that was actually a clear indication of where I was headed. And probably the most significant dark influence on me was the music I listened to. Some music may have words that seem harmless—mindless, in fact—but when these words are paired with musical combinations that have a dark spiritual form, they have power to create more darkness in the minds of those of us who hear them. We can "feel" whether the tones in a particular piece are created of light or of darkness by how the music reacts with our own spirit to create a mood. The music I chose at that time lulled me into a stupor, preaching death and selfishness in symbolic phrases, and it crowded out the light.

Even then, I knew that the music I loved and the things that had become important to me were not "of God." But at the time I was convinced that I was spiritually defective. I thought I was a failure in the eyes of God, and so I became just that, embracing the darkness. I thought that I was in control of my life, not recognizing that the damaging power I was tapping into was in reality controlling me. Darkness creates unsteadiness and uncertainty within us. As the level of light drops within us, we vacillate in what we perceive as the best course. We often want things or conditions in our lives to change in ways that are not good for us, for the lifestyles that are composed of darkness are alluring and deceptive. At the time of my suicide, I loved my family, but I wasn't willing to fight the darkness, to live a difficult life in order to be with them. I had tumbled into spiritual free-fall.

The only way I could have saved myself then would have been to purge myself of darkness and replenish my spirit with light. I saw my problems as being so massive that there was no remedy strong enough to help me, but what I hadn't understood is that it is the direction that I was traveling that was destroying me. There are only two directions: toward light or toward darkness. It doesn't matter where we are on the road, as long as we are moving toward that light. Each step, however small, is significant. I was told that it is the little things that we do that have so much power because they spread and grow and continue to breed.

At that time it didn't even occur to me that I could pray. People often pray as a last resort, after they have stumbled around in the darkness long enough to get desperate for help from a God they usually don't acknowledge. But I was so ridden with guilt that I didn't dare face my maker, although that's precisely what I needed to do.

God has incredible power to organize darkness and light with His thoughts alone. When we come to Him in humble supplication, with powerful, prayerful words of light, darkness is forced out. It is replaced with healing truth, with light, which then gives us the ability to see more light. God, being without darkness, cannot give us darkness. He can only provide us with truth, with what is best for us. All of God's answers are contained in light, and it is through this light that God transmits pure knowledge to us. Truth is unchanging. Either we accept it and are enlightened, or we reject it and remain in darkness.

That is why it is never the "least" we can do to pray. When we pray to God with true purpose, with faith and a desire for truth, we create the most powerful extensions of light that we are capable of. Many times we don't see the positive impact that our prayers have on the lives of those we pray for, though every prayer uttered is heard by God. We fluctuate in our ability to see and hear His responses to us, but He is always communicating to us. I often pray for the other spirits that were confined in the place of darkness. I pray that they, too, will see God, who is reaching out to each one of them.

We are, all of us, eternal creatures with endless potential. God the Father told me that He Himself had had a mortal existence on a world like ours and had progressed along a path by choosing good over evil. These words came as a surprise to me. This pattern of advancing spiritually by choosing good has been going on forever and will continue forever. I was told that there are countless worlds revolving around countless suns, and each is inhabited by children of God, who are subject to these same laws.

And since we are eternal creatures, there is no such thing as ultimate and total death. We die to live again, but where we live again depends on how we conduct our mortal lives. The more we are willing to love, the more light we create within ourselves. The more we err, the more darkness we propagate. All of God's blessings are conditional, for God's laws are immutable. These laws cannot be abrogated or set aside with impunity. When we violate them, there is a punishment involved, a decrease in light. When we obey them, there follows a blessing, an increase in light. These are realities.

I was also told that as a woman I was half of a whole entity. It is the union of a man and a woman that gives us procreative power, which is the most God-like power that we are allowed to assume as mortal beings. I was told that my husband and I are of equal importance in that union but that we have different roles to perform. We are born with particular attributes, aside from differing physical endowments, that are gifts from God to help us perform these roles. I was told that as a mother who chose to stay home with Alex and Jacob, I was doing more than

I knew to provide my children with security and positive feelings about themselves. Many mothers can't be with their children full time, but I could; and so to sacrifice a career for motherhood was one of the few major decisions I made in those years that were good. In exchange for accepting my responsibilities as a mother and wife, I would receive opportunities to grow and to learn lessons that are closely tied to the duties that come with my gender.

Then I recognized that Richard wasn't out earning a living because he loves doing it. Instead, he was doing it because he loves us. As the masculine half of our union, he would also be given opportunities to learn lessons of life that are innately linked to his role as a father, a husband, and a man. God gave men certain powers not so they could be rulers or tyrants but rather to teach them about sacrifice and responsibility. Service, not rank and privilege, is God's intention for men.

The seeds of other truths were also planted in me, though I would not be able to cultivate them then. I recognized that they would sprout throughout the course of my life and that I would be able to harvest understanding. What I learned the day I died was how to learn.

EIGHTEEN

N ow my perception was shifting, and the darkness seemed to lift slightly. When I first entered the dark prison, my vision took in only the things and the people in the realm of darkness. But once I had taken enough light in from God and Jesus, my spiritual eyes were opened to another dimension in the darkness. Now I could see that beings of light were all around me.

At first I could only feel their presence. Pockets of energy brushed past, almost like quick breezes. I could feel the light coming from these spirits before I was able to see their forms. Once I recognized that beings of light were whipping about, once I felt them, I found that I could see them. I had traded in the doctrine of man, "seeing is believing," for the truth of God, "believing is seeing."

These spirit messengers of God glowed pleasantly

without God's solid form and majestic power. They were dressed in white robes, and I could not tell whether they were male or female. Although I could not see what they were doing as they rushed here and there, I knew that they were assisting those of us on earth. Like oil over water, the active layer of spirits of light rested above a layer of grim, motionless dark beings.

Drifting onto the plane, the newly deceased were dressed in white robes, but their gowns were dingy. Like silent sleep-walkers, these spellbound souls descended into the darkness, arms to their sides, their expressionless eyes locked in empty gazes. They came from the same direction that I had, dull and hopeless casualties of life that had banked on true death, continuing to fill in the back edge of the prison as the darkness expanded to accommodate them. So sad, they were so young and so dead. As I watched them filing in by the dozens, I was told that most of us who are dying now are going to a place of darkness.

Hell, while also a specific dimension, is primarily a state of mind. When we die, we are bound by what we think. In mortality the more solid our thoughts become, as we act upon them—allowing darkness to develop in others and in ourselves—the more damning they are. I had been in Hell long before I died, and I hadn't realized it because I had escaped many of the consequences up until the point that I took my life. But when we die, our state of mind grows far more obvious because we are gathered together with those who think as we do. This ordering is completely natural and is consistent with how we choose to live while we are in this world. Our time is but a heartbeat in the eternal scheme of creation, and yet it is the crucial moment of truth, the turning point. It determines how our spirits will exist forever, into both the future and the past.

I was becoming less and less a part of the place of darkness with each particle of light that I accepted. I hadn't felt myself lift off the surface, but now I was hovering above the field of darkness, into the realm of the scurrying spirits of light. I must have realized then that I was about to return to life, for I was afraid. I still doubted that I could endure life without doing irreparable harm to others. But I was told emphatically that my past—being hurt so badly throughout my life and also hurting Richard and the boys, in particular—didn't matter now. All I had to do from then on, I was told, was to obey the commandments. It was simple. We all are obedient. It is simply a matter of whom we obey.

I could feel the urgency in the spirits who were scurrying about to do the work of God. I was then told that we are in the final moments before the Savior will return to the earth. I was told that the war between darkness and light upon the earth has grown so intense that if we are not continually seeking light, the darkness will consume us and we will be lost. I was not told when it would happen, but I understood that the earth is being prepared for the Second Coming of Christ. I looked down at the pathetic souls and realized that I no longer felt as they did. I wanted to live.

Then the powerful energy source that had transported me to the dark prison returned to liberate me. For a split second a rushing sensation engulfed me. The darkness sped past, and suddenly I was back in my body, lying on the couch. As I filled my lungs with air, I was suddenly reminded of physical pain; my stomach ached and my head throbbed, and I felt heavy and weak again. But I was overcome with humble gratitude. I felt like Ebenezer Scrooge, having been granted a warning glimpse of my fate; and then once I understood, having been granted a second chance.

NINETEEN

The front door swung open, filling the living room with welcome light. The sheer drape caught the breeze, a counterpoint to Richard's heavy stride as he made his way down the hallway. His silhouette diffused the bright sunlight. The effects of the drugs I had taken were apparent as I swung my feet to the ground, pulling my body up to a sitting position. Walking into the living room, Richard perched on the arm of the love seat, and I said to him, "You are never going to believe this."

His stunned look of concern at my condition told me that he just might.

Despite my excitement, my speech was slow and thick as I tried to tell him gently of the horrible thing I had done. He must have sensed that I was in dire straits because he just nodded at the news. His face was white as he moved from the arm of the love seat to the couch. "Are you okay? Shouldn't we take you to the hospital?" he asked.

But God was still speaking to me through His light. I knew that it was not necessary. God had restored me to life. And I knew that it would do more harm than good. Since I was a dependent wife of an Air Force officer, the military had the power to ship me back to the States. It would be hard to convince them that I was no longer a threat to myself, and what my family needed most now was to be together. I'd have to sweat out the drugs, but I wasn't going to be permanently affected. "Look at me, Richard," I told him. "I'm fine. It would be a disaster to bring the chain of command into this."

Once he got over his initial shock, I told him of my journey. As I recounted my experience, the first thing I noticed was that most of my restored memories had been taken from me. All I could remember were the very first memories of birth and being cradled by my mother and a few highlights from my early childhood in the new, expanded form. But for the rest of the events of my life, the details that remained with me were those that had existed in my mind before I died. Even those memories seemed a little blunted, like information I'd learned in textbooks years ago. I could remember the broad outlines, but not many of the facts.

As I began telling Richard about my journey to the world of dark spirits, I realized that the ability to see darkness and light remained with me. I could see little pieces of energy everywhere. I felt as though I could put my hand through the wall, and the molecules would part if it was my will. My potted plants had a visible glow to them. Richard had a great aura of energy about him.

Seeing this energy, I could feel the presence of God in

everything in the room. I could see that every object's purpose was to worship God through serving us—the books, the bookcase, the pillows propped on the couch and love seat. Everything was answering God's voice and praising Him on its own level. And I realized that this energy was their true essence, that their physicality was much less significant than the light they contained.

Now I opened up to Richard for the first time in many years and told him how I had been feeling unable to control my behavior. At once the words I needed to say came to me with crystal clarity. The moment I spoke the words, light filled my spirit. I suddenly realized how long I had been imprisoned and why.

Just as God and Jesus Christ are real, a being of darkness, Satan, truly exists. He has conclaves of dark angels, and we are their prey. These dark spirits, I understood, had surrounded me and had run rampant in my home, affecting my entire family. It was all so clear to me now. I was the one who had invited them in to promote their chaos and contention. I had been so filled with darkness that I denied the evil company I was keeping.

I could see that the music I had loved had been directly inspired by Satan and his angels, that the heavy, brooding melodies and pulsing beats had been almost constantly filling my mind with darkness. Antitruth messages had been pumped into me, influencing my thoughts and behavior. And I had not only listened, I had danced.

Then the door swung open again. "Mama, are you better now?" came my sweet Alex's voice. Jacob's golden hair bounced as he came toddling in behind Alex and flopped himself across my lap. I scooped him up as Alex wrapped his arms around my neck. I held my boys tight and silently prayed, "Thank you."

My friend Jennifer trailed in after the boys and stopped in her tracks when she saw me. "Angie, you look terrible," she said. "Is there anything I can do? Should I take the boys for you?"

"No, I'm okay, but I have to talk to you," I said. As Richard took the boys into the kitchen to make lunch, Jennifer helped me climb the stairs.

We sat on my bed together as she studied my scarred wrists. Then I told her about my experience. Hugging me, she said, "This is incredible. Are you okay? You should have called me."

"I know, I know, I can't believe I would do something so stupid!" I said.

She urged me to go to the hospital, but I refused, explaining my fear that I'd be shipped back.

"Yeah, you're probably right. And it would somehow get into Richard's permanent record that he had a psycho wife."

Then as I continued to fill her in on the details of my journey, I was flooded with new revelations. I could see even more clearly that I had been Satan's puppet. While opposites exist—light and darkness, truth and deception, love and hate—there are also myriad possibilities in between, contortions and distortions of the truth that are made of darkness. To love is the most important thing we come into this world to learn, yet Satan had twisted this simple truth to persuade me to perform a terrible act of darkness in the name of love for my husband and children. How could it be love that prompted me to leave them, without even fully considering how it might affect them to discover my dead body in the house? Suicide was the most selfish act that I could ever have been capable of. It was an act of vanity, stemming from the belief that I couldn't open up to anyone, that I had to solve my problems on my own. These were Satan's lies.

God loves us and calls to us. He cannot force us to choose light.

As I reflected on these things, a powerful energy rose in me, confirming that my new insights were true. And the revelations continued: I now saw that I was never forced to come to this earth. I could see that before my birth, I knew what I would face, and that with God, I had co-authored the course of my life. I knew that confusion and heartache would be my companions. I chose my parents and even several of my friends before I came to earth. The option to have an easier life was always mine, but I volunteered, I sacrificed, because I loved the people who were to become my family and I wanted to be with them. I knew what to expect, and still I chose to come. We all make that choice.

I also realized that, even when I was far beyond God's touch, He had been sending helpers to me. A Sunday school teacher had taught my son to pray, and because of the faith of my four-year-old, my family had survived when many don't. I never met that woman, and she probably has no idea of the good that her simple act of charity—teaching little boys and girls for an hour a week—has done. Yet the results of her small kindness will undoubtedly be felt forever.

Later I would see clear evidence of those results. A year or so after my suicide attempt, Alex and Jacob were watching an animated movie called *Watership Down*. There is a rabbit in the story who has a vision that something terrible is going to happen if all the rabbits don't leave their warren right away. Alex didn't understand why the rabbit was rolling on the ground, so Richard explained what a vision was. Alex then said, "I have visions sometimes. Not all the time, though." I gently corrected him, telling him the difference between imagining the future and having a vision of it. "No," Alex replied. "I had a vision when we were still living in America. I saw that we were going someplace far away where there was a church, and friends, and a new place that would make our family be okay." Now Richard chimed in to remind him that he had a vivid imagination, which was not the same as a vision. But Alex stood firm. "I *did* have a vision. I saw lots of people singing," he said. In that moment I felt a burst of energy and the certainty that his words were true. The "new place" Alex had seen was Okinawa, which had become a sacred healing ground for my family. It was here that my truest friends came into my life. It was the support of the congregation of our church—probably the source of the "singing" Alex saw—that gave me strength and faith.

■

What God and His Son taught me on my journey didn't make me perfect. I have continued to struggle over the years. This life is hard. It's supposed to be hard, but I am a far more attentive student now. In the years since my experience, I have engaged in a continuous and intense study of the Word of God. I try to seek out that which is made of light, surrounding myself with music that opens my mind to the spirit of God. I seek forgiveness from those I have offended so that they may be less inclined to be hindered by my weakness. I kneel in prayer often and find that when I am receptive, it can bring me reassurance, showing me that the pain in life has a purpose. Suffering is often the price we pay so that we might have the desire to help others. When this motivation to give of ourselves leads to action, our service to other people is exchanged for an increase in light. The manifestation of this light is true happiness and peace.

I can see the effects of increased light in my family, which are often revealed quite poignantly. For example, each night before I tuck Alex in bed, we kneel together to pray. One particular night something was bothering him, and I asked him what was wrong.

"Mama," he said, "how come I can't see God?"

"God lives in Heaven," I explained, "but that doesn't mean He isn't with you all of the time."

"Well, what if you have something really important that you need?" he asked.

"That's what we are doing when we pray, Alex. We're talking to God. You can tell Him what your problem is and ask for His help, and He'll give it to you."

After some prying I finally learned that he needed help in dealing with a boy in the neighborhood who had been picking on him.

"He hits me with sticks and calls me names," Alex confessed. "He won't let me play with other kids either." Then he started to cry.

Jacob toddled in and headed for the toybox.

"Let me put Jacob down in his room, and then we'll talk about it, okay, sweetheart?" I said as I scooped Jacob up.

"Okay, Mama."

A few minutes after I sat down in the rocking chair with Jacob, I could hear Alex getting up, his sheets rustling briefly as he slipped out of bed. As Jacob drifted off to sleep, I could hear Alex praying reverently.

He had climbed back in bed by the time I successfully laid Jacob in his crib. "So how did it go?" I asked.

"Just fine," he said. "God told me that I should pray for

Jerome, that whoever is being mean to him will stop. He said that I should come and get you when Jerome is being mean to me."

The Spirit whispered an assurance that my son had truly received an answer to his prayer.

TWENTY

I've seen tremendous changes within myself as a result of opening my spirit to God's light. I deal with challenges with new hope and confidence. I know now that I can choose my destiny rather than allow events of the past to direct my life.

Once I moved beyond the darkness into the light, it became obvious to me that it was fear that kept me in Satan's clutches throughout my years of abuse. One residue of this fear was a terrible self-consciousness. Fear of being laughed at and fear of mediocrity convinced me to hide my God-given talents.

One of those talents is the ability to sing, which I share with my sister, Toni. We had performed a duet that went poorly during a Sunday church service. When we stood up to sing, I got a nervous twitch in my cheek that she thought was quite humorous. Being as nervous as I was, she burst out in uncontrollable laughter. As Toni hunched over trying to compose herself, I had to warble alone through the most humiliating two minutes of my young life. After that I decided I would never sing in public again.

A year or so after my experience with death, a close friend who loved music with a passion equal to mine discovered me singing along with an opera while I was cleaning the house. A talented violinist, she persuaded me to prepare a duet with her to be performed at church. For months we practiced, and I procrastinated. At last I worked up the courage to schedule our performance, taking consolation from the fact that my friend would also be on display. And guess what? It went well!

As a result I was asked to sing at a special church service with the warning that I wouldn't have a chance to rehearse with the pianist until the evening of the event. I hesitated but eventually agreed.

Well, everything went wrong that night. Both the accompanist and I were late, and our practice session was horrendous. She kept hitting wrong notes, and my voice was pinched with nervousness. When it was time to begin, I had a huge lump in my throat and a stomach tight with tension. Silently I pleaded with God to help me calm down enough to do a good job. No relief came.

Finally I leaned over to whisper to the church leader that I just couldn't sing that night. But then a voice came into my mind, saying, "It would have been selfish of you to say no." Suddenly I was filled with calm reassurance, and I sang almost as comfortably as if I were at home doing the dishes.

Around that time I was once again gripped by the cycle. As early as a few months after my experience with death, long-suppressed memories of my childhood came flooding back in, threatening my new security. I thought that surely I would die from the pain as these visions of my childhood came back to me. As I reacted to the parade of injustices, I could feel the prodding of my past—dependencies, the urge to escape—and I began to fear for my spiritual welfare. It was pure agony for me because I knew that I had to pass through the pain of these memories, but this time to rely on God. It took all of the energy I possessed to be strong as I endured the waves of past and present anguish.

I waited until my family had all gone to bed so that I could have some privacy before I opened the Scriptures. The words that usually brought me soothing comfort barely touched this gaping wound in my emotions. After pouring out my heart in prayer for help and guidance, I went to bed, where I lay awake, next to my sleeping husband, sobbing into my pillow. I was yearning to feel the love and security that had filled me so completely during my visit with God the Father and His Son, Jesus Christ, when suddenly I felt a tiny hand gently pat me on the back. A quiet peace filled me. I believe that the touch came from a messenger of light, who had been trying to comfort me for many years. But only then, in that moment of humble supplication, had I been within reach.

The undeniable truth that I now know with certainty is that death is but a passing. It is a momentary change. There is suffering and anger so thick in our troubled world that for some it is almost unbearable, but the moment we cross into the next life, the pain of this world dissipates. It's like waking up from a nightmare. What seemed so real and terrifying is gone and forgotten in a moment, unless we take matters into our own hands. Then it's like waking up to find that the monsters are real. Hell is real and far, far more terrifying than we can comprehend.

The absolute, all-encompassing love that I felt when I

stood there within the light taught me that, regardless of what we must pass through, life is good. It is the gift of God, who loves us. He sustains us with words of encouragement, but we must be open to hearing Him. He sends messengers—people and spirits—who can help us, but we must recognize them.

Immediately after my experience I sought qualified, enlightened, professional help. Mercifully, my counselor didn't dismiss my experience as a hallucination. He understood the power of darkness and of light. For the gentle and supportive guidance he provided me in overcoming the ravages of darkness in my life, I will be forever grateful.

Ultimately it was personal tragedy that taught me to love—to give. Through my trials I have developed strengths and talents that have enabled me to help those around me. It shocks me to think that I had come so perilously close to surrendering that which was most precious to me, to have risked damaging my loved ones' destinies, to have threatened them with the same darkness in which I had imprisoned my spirit. Today, every day when I wake up, I am filled with happiness that I was given another chance at life, with such profound gratitude that I was taught to transform despair into hope and truth and light. This, not the absence of pain, is true joy.

EPILOGUE

In the years since that January when I took my life, I have felt inspired to share my story with a few close friends from time to time, though in general I have kept this most sacred experience to myself. But a few months after I returned to the States from Okinawa, I began to notice a dangerous trend. Marvelous stories of the love and light that greeted those who ventured into death and returned to tell of it were the subject of almost every talk show. Those accounts have greatly increased our knowledge of the "life beyond life," and I am grateful that many have had the courage to share their experience. Yet at the same time we have been seeing political figures, rock stars, doctors, and even children embracing suicide as a kind of heroic exit from this world. I began to fear that if people didn't hear the other side of the near-death experience, they might interpret these marvelous accounts to mean that suicide could bring release from their problems.

As I learned, nothing could be further from the truth.

Still I resisted telling my story, recognizing that some people would view it with skepticism and even suspicion, as well as the fact that it would require me to reveal some of the most painful and private details of my life. In time, however, I found it impossible to remain silent.

I hope that through my experience, people will be able to take comfort in the fact that death is but a passing—that we are eternal and we will live forever. And I hope that they will recognize that there are only two directions we can take: Either we must progress out of our imperfect existence here, or we will take our earthly baggage with us. One way or another we all must learn the hard lessons of life. Finally, it is my fervent wish that all who read this book will find in it a source of hope and will find courage to live. For as I have had the privilege of seeing with my own eyes, God is with us always. The Scriptures tell us, "Though I walk through the valley of the shadow of death . . . Thou art with me." Even through the ultimate darkness, if we are only willing to believe, none of us need ever walk alone.